THE TWINS
FREE AT LAST

THE TWINS
FREE AT LAST

KATE KRAY

JOHN BLAKE

Published by John Blake Publishing Ltd,
3 Bramber Court, 2 Bramber Road, London W14 9PB, England

First published in hardback in Great Britain in 2000

ISBN 1 903402 25 5

British Library Cataloguing-in-Publication Data:
A catalogue record for this book is available from
the British Library.

Typeset by Jon Davies

Printed in England by CPD, Wales

1 3 5 7 9 10 8 6 4 2

Papers used by Blake Publishing Ltd are natural, recyclable products
made from wood grown in sustainable forests. The manufacturing processes
conform to the environmental regulations of the country of origin.

DEDICATION

Reggie and Ronnie Kray —
love 'em or loathe 'em, they were Britain's most
notorious gangsters. This book is dedicated
to all the loyal friends that stood by them
throughout their many years of incarceration.

ACKNOWLEDGEMENTS

Reg and Ron's real friends for being so honest, especially,
Charlie Walker and Linda Calvey.

Ronnie's little darling – Chantel Binns.

David Bailey for the fantastic photo.

Chester Stern and Paul Field from the *Mail on Sunday*.

Adam Parfitt for the hard work and headaches he endured.

Thank you.

CONTENTS

FOREWORD

It has been five long years since Ron died. My life has moved on, I've written a number one bestseller, and I now have my own TV series on Channel 5. So when I was asked to write this book, I was very, very reluctant.

I telephoned Joey Pyle, one of Ron's oldest friends, for some advice. Joey is a shrewd man and always puts me right. Joe told me not to write the book: leave their memories in peace.

I almost put my pen down and stopped writing that moment. He was echoing the very thoughts that had been going through my head the moment I started work. But then I sat down and thought about it. I thought about everything that had been written about Ron and Reg in the past, so much of it crap from people who had never met them —

The Twins: Free at Last

hearsay, half truths, sometimes just plain lies. Even if the twins had lived to be a hundred, they would never have managed to collect the number of minders, drivers and associates that seem to have crawled out of the woodwork. It seemed to me that everyone had had their pound of flesh from the Krays. Only a handful of people knew the real Ron and Reg. I was lucky – I was married to Ron and even five years after hes death, people still ask me questions. Were they really as vicious as everyone said? Why did they stay in prison so long? What? Why? Where? When?

So I decided to carry on with my work. I feel that if I can give an honest, no-nonsense account of what I know, then Ron and Reg Kray can be left in peace. I don't want to glorify them like some soppy bird seeing them through rose-tinted glasses – they were vicious men, and I know that. But they were a big part of my life for a long time and if by writing this book I can put the record straight once and for all, then so be it.

I'd like to think that this will be the last thing ever written about them. Somehow I doubt it will be...

Kate Kray
London, October 2000

PROLOGUE

*'I'd rather die standing than on my knees,
begging to be released.'*

Ronnie Kray

I woke up with a start. For a moment I had no idea where I was. I remember looking at the small alarm clock that stands on the bedside table. It was 3.35 am. I took a sip of water and lay back down. Then, suddenly, I saw my dad standing in front of me. He looked young. He was wearing his checked overcoat, the one he always wore when I was a child. I didn't understand. I was puzzled because my father had died a year before. I studied my dad's lovely face. I remember clearly asking, 'What are you doing here, Dad?'

Dad smiled. A familiar smile. One that I had missed so much.

The Twins: Free at Last

'I wanted to see you,' he answered.

I was puzzled. 'But you are dead.'

Dad smiled and explained. He said that, yes, he was dead, but he never left me. He said that when I suddenly start thinking of him, for no reason at all, that's when he is with me. I can't usually see him but, he said, he makes himself felt inside my head.

I asked him, 'How come I can see you now?'

He answered, 'Because you are dead, too.'

At first I was shocked, then I was glad. I was with my father and I loved him.

I wanted to kiss him but I was afraid to, in case he got upset. Before his death he used to cry over the slightest little thing. But dad was happy.

' No … no, it's all right, nobody cries here.'

So I put my arms around him and cuddled him tight. I have always maintained that is what arms are for — cuddling.

Then I saw Ron. He looked great. He was wearing a Prince of Wales checked suit. His hair was jet black. I gasped, 'Ron. You look brilliant. You look so young.'

He didn't look like the Ron I knew. He looked more like the glamorous photos I had seen of him. He laughed and explained that after death, if a spirit wants to return to their loved ones, then they usually manifest themselves in the form of when they were at their happiest. In his case, it was in the 1960s. But Ron being Ron, he wanted me to pass on a message to Reggie. I promised that I would. He said, 'Tell Reggie that I'm all right and that it is smashin' here.'

He insisted that I got the message right. As usual.

At that point, my dad told me that it was time I went back. He said that it wasn't my time yet. I didn't want to go. I wanted to stay with Ron and my dad. They said that it wasn't possible. I miss my dad so much and I know he loved me. I was his little girl and I remember that whenever I went out in the evening when I was a teenager, my dad would always leave the landing light on until I got home safely.

Dad smiled at me. He looked at peace.

'I'll leave a light on in heaven for you,' he said.

I kissed him goodbye. Then I kissed Ron.

I opened my eyes and I was back in my bed again. I sat up in bed. I wasn't frightened. I felt calm but wide awake.

I always knew that it would take death to free Ron and Reg. How could it have been otherwise? No criminal in the history of Britain was more famous. They were celebrities. They were friends with members of the government; even members of the royal family could be seen in their clubs.

I've been asked so many times, why were they never freed? The answer is simple: they got too close. Too close to the establishment; too close to becoming untouchable. Even when they were nicked they knew it was coming. Why? Because Lord Boothby, a peer of the realm and good 'friend' of Ronnie, tipped them off.

If they had continued to get away with it for another couple of years, perhaps they would have become untouchable. They would have been so far removed from

The Twins: Free at Last

the crimes they committed it would have been impossible to trace anything back to them. Even in their heyday, Ron could walk into a pub, kill George Cornell, and tell everyone he'd done it, safe in the knowledge that nobody could touch him for it.

The twins set the standard for organised crime in Britain. They were glamorous and nobody, before or since has achieved the same level of sophistication. Look at the gangs nowadays. They don't have the profile or the glamour of the Krays. Not a chance. Their crimes were vicious, yes; some would say barbaric. Even in prison, Ron could strike fear into the hearts of the toughest men around him. In Parkhurst one time, he was sitting having his dinner with a bunch of other cons, when somebody noticed he hadn't eaten his greens.

'Not eating your greens then, Ron?' asked the con. Ron was silent for a few seconds, then he lifted up his metal tray and with a single sweep used it to slice off the con's nose.

But it wasn't their violent nature that sealed their fate. The bottom line was that they were far too famous...

When I was married to Ron, I used to visit him or phone him every day. I talked to him about being free all the time, and he always used to say, 'Don't worry about me Kate. Just help Reggie get free.' Ron knew he belonged in Broadmoor. He knew he needed his medication. If he was feeling ill in the head, he'd say to me, 'Kate, I can't see you for a few days.' He was sensible like that. All he wanted was for Reggie to get out.

Prologue

By the time Reg was freed, he only had a few weeks to live. In my eyes, that was no act of kindness; that was an act of cruelty, to say to a dying man, 'This is what you've missed for the last 32 years; now you're dying, so you'll never have it.'

Not that it would have bothered Reg. I can hear him now, being told he was going to be let out: 'About fucking time, too!' And he'd have been right. They could have released Reggie years ago, and if they had I'd have known where to find him every day: in Broadmoor by Ronnie's side, not on the streets causing trouble. Reg would never have gone back into organised crime.

Ron, on the other hand, was a different matter. I asked him once what was the one thing he'd do if he was freed. I don't know what I was expecting him to say – go down the East End, perhaps, have a drink with some friends. No. The one thing he wanted to do was to have a walk in the park and stroke a dog. After he's shot three people, that is!

I spent so long talking to Ron, and Reg too – that was all we could do – talk. So much crap has been written about them, I think it's time, now that they are gone, to set the record straight. In this book you will find stories about Ron and Reg from my time with them, but also tributes and anecdotes from members of the firm and others who knew them closely.

I want to tell the truth about them. They were violent men. Nobody knew that better than me. I'll never forget the time Ron had the hump with me, and he told a friend of his, Mick, to kill me. Mick laughed and said,

The Twins: Free at Last

'Ron, you've got more chance of me killing you than Kate.' Next time I went to see him after that, of course, I was all cocky – 'Ha, you see, even Mick won't kill me!'

Ron just held my hand and said in his quiet voice, 'No, Kate. If I wanted to kill you, I'd just ask one of the nutters in here to do it on their home leave. They'd do anything for me.' That soon wiped a smile from my face.

I've been on a visit with Ron and a couple of faces, and one of the guys would say something that upset Ron. You would never have known it to look at him. He just kept smiling and said, 'I want you to leave now, 'cos I want to have a word with Kate.' They shook hands, and the geezer left thinking Ron was his best mate. Then Ron turned to the other face, and with a glint in his eye and in his quietest voice, he said, simply, 'Kill him.'

And in the next breath he'd change his mind. But that was Ron.

Oh, he could be a nasty bastard, alright, and he knew it. But there was a softer side to him that few people ever saw. Sometimes on a visit I'd start crying, and Ron would never quite know what to do. He'd wipe the tears off my face, and nine times out of ten he'd end up wiping the mascara everywhere so I looked like a panda. Then he'd send me off to the bathroom to compose myself. When I came back, he'd apologise and say, 'It's the German in me, Kate. I'm sorry.' Kray was a German name, you see.

I don't want to pretend that they weren't violent men. But there was far more to them than that. When you think about it, they were just a couple of ragamuffins from the East End who did something with their life. Show me a person who hasn't heard of the Kray twins. It takes a certain kind of tenacity to become that famous, but at the end of the day they could hardly even read or write. Imagine what they would have achieved if they'd been educated...

I hope this book presents a rounded portrait of Ron and Reg Kray. When I used to talk to Ron, he'd tell me all his secrets, and say, 'Pay attention, Kate. One day all this will make a good subject for one of your books.' So much of what he told me I had to keep quiet until him and Reg had passed away. But I know they wanted the truth to be told. Now, at last, it can be.

REG ON RON

*R*on is a very complex character, often contradictory, sometimes eccentric. I've known him to be vicious when necessary, but deep down he has a very kind nature. Anyone who has met Ron will confirm that he has an immaculate dress sense and is always the perfect gentleman.

One time Ron and I were in the Greengate public house and Ron was sitting on a bar stool, three fellas entered the bar and stood directly behind Ron making sarcastic remarks against him. I watched and listened, but before I could make a move, Ron stepped down off the stool. He hit one of the fellas with a right hand punch. He hit the floor immediately like a windless bagpipe.

Ron hit another with a right then a left, sending him to the floor. The third joker looked on in amazement. His face went white. He apologized and made for the exit.

Ron was completely fearless.

THE FINAL
NIGHT OF
FREEDOM

The Twins demanded loyalty and respect. Even after they were banged up. And they had the power to see that that loyalty was respected. Even from prison, the Krays had a very, very long arm …

Thirty years after their heyday, they had a core of followers who treated them with the respect they demanded. One of those men was Charlie. Throughout the sixties, Charlie was at their side. He is a man of his word. A proud man, and one I am proud to have as my friend. He has an air of confidence about him and you know instantly it wouldn't be a wise move to cross him.

He is a big, broad man, and he knows how to act with everyone. He's always suited and booted, and when Charlie is in the room you know about it — he stands out like an immovable object.

The Twins: Free at Last

It was in the summer of 1988 when Ron asked me to phone Charlie to arrange a visit. He was such a friendly man that we clicked immediately. In those early days, I have to put my hands up and admit that I was green and didn't know the score. I was always eager to please Ron. I tried to do all the things he wanted but it was impossible.

There was always so much to do. So many messages to deliver, so many people to see and places to go. It seemed that Ron had completely taken over my life and there was no time left for me any more.

Charlie sensed that and encouraged me to slow down. I am pleased to say that I took his advice and, since then, he has phoned me every week without fail, not for anything in particular, just to see if things are OK and if I need anything.

He loved Ronnie Kray, that was obvious, and when Ron died he was devastated. I remember when I was paying my last respects to Ron at the funeral parlour which was under siege by TV crews, journalists from all over the world and thousands of fans all wanting to see Ron for the last time. Grim-looking men with broken noses and wearing cashmere overcoats surrounded the Chapel of Rest.

Reggie had control of who was allowed in and who wasn't. He had made a list of names in order of priority.

Obviously, Reggie went first to pay his respects. Charlie Kray was second on the list, and I was third. Unless your name was on that list, you could forget it.

Charlie arrived while I was with Ron. I had so much

The Final Night of Freedom

I wanted to tell Ron, but a gentle knock on the door broke my thoughts.

'Sorry to disturb you, Kate, but there is a man at the door called Charlie. He said you know him.'

I was so pleased that it was Charlie; I needed to see a familiar face.

Charlie was shown into the Chapel of Rest. He looked pale and drawn — it was obvious he had been crying but he managed to keep his grief under control. He put his arms around me and hugged me tight. His huge arms engulfed me. It was a great comfort. Slowly, he peered into the oak coffin, the brass handles shining in the sunlight coming through the window.

Flowers, mainly spring flowers, were everywhere and their scent filled the air. Ron's body looked like a cold marble statue. Charlie bent forward and gently kissed Ron's forehead. Tears welled up in his eyes, and there was genuine pain etched on his tough face, a face that had seen many a brawl in its day. Finally, he broke down and cried.

I didn't know how to comfort him. I just didn't have the words. It nearly broke my heart. I've heard it said that tough men don't cry. Well that day, I saw a tough man cry for his friend. The man he describes as 'a diamond'.

Charlie has held his peace about Ron and Reg for thirty years. Even now it took some persuasion to get him to speak about the two men he respected above all others. But after Reg's death I went to see him, to talk about the twins and reminisce about the old times. And he told me stories I'd never even heard before...

The Twins: Free at Last

Charlie got to know the twins through two brothers – Checa and Teddy Berry. He was a good friend of the Berrys, two tough men who didn't like the twins one little bit. It was only a matter of time before the brothers would end up having a row.

And boy, did they have a row! Ron went right into one and shot Teddy in the leg. Now normally, if you do someone in the leg, you get them to remove their trousers, otherwise the material from the trousers makes the gunshot wound go septic. Well, Ron didn't bother with any of that. The wound turned bad and Teddy had to have his leg amputated.

Ron felt terrible – but not as terrible as Teddy! The row was over something really stupid, and it certainly didn't warrant somebody losing their leg. Ron had just lost his temper.

The twins tried to put things straight by arranging a big party for Teddy at the York Hall up in the East End of London. It was a fantastic evening, and Ron and Reg made sure that everyone who was anyone attended. They even raised enough money to buy Teddy a pub called the Bridge House just off Bow Common Lane. Checa and Teddy took over the pub, were good hosts and the whole thing was a roaring success.

Things quietened down for a bit between Teddy and Ron. But deep down the Berry brothers still resented the twins, and in particular Ronnie. Well, it's not surprising, I suppose – he had shot the geezer in the leg!

They barred them from the pub. Well, maybe barred is the wrong word – you didn't really bar the twins from

The Final Night of Freedom

anywhere – but let's just say that they made it known that they were not welcome. I suppose it was reasonable under the circumstances. Charlie didn't really know the twins at the time. He'd seen them around, of course, and he knew who they were, but so did everybody, unless they came from another planet or something.

Then, one night, right out of the blue, Teddy changed his mind and said that the twins could come to the pub, and they would be made welcome. The Bridge House was Charlie's local. He always drank in there, and when the twins eventually visited the pub, it was as if nothing had happened. Everyone was friends again. That's how it often was in those days – you never knew what was going on behind the scenes.

So that's how Charlie got to know the twins. At the time, he worked for a bloke called Micky who owned a car front, selling all kinds of cars. The twins would turn up at the front and just help themselves to whatever car they fancied – normally a Standard Vanguard for Reg and a Yank for Ron. Not that either of them could drive, of course, but they had people to drive them around anyway. So they'd turn up, help themselves to the cars they wanted, drive them around till they ran out of petrol, and just dump them on the side of the road, or in a ditch, or wherever they felt like it. Next day, you could bet your bottom dollar they'd be back at Micky's garage helping themselves to another motor!

The twins were used to getting what they wanted, and one day they decided that what they wanted was Micky's own motor, a rather swanky Chevrolet Impala. Of

The Twins: Free at Last

course, being Ron and Reg, Micky couldn't say no. Later that night Charlie was driving back to the front with his boss one evening, when what should they see but a Chevvy Impala crashed into a big hole in the road, the back of the car sticking up in the air, and two blokes in suits peering down the hole, scratching their heads.

Micky did a double-take. 'Hang on, I recognise that car.'

'Leave it, Micky,' said Charlie.

'That's my Chevvy! Someone's crashed my fucking Chevvy!'

'Yeah, and that's Ron and Reg,' laughed Charlie. 'Believe me, you don't want to get involved. Forget about your motor.'

Micky had no choice but to write the motor off. It proved to be one of the more sensible things he did, and from that moment on, Micky's garage was under the protection of Ron and Reg. Sure, he had to supply them with cars, but that was a small price to pay for being under the wing of the twins. It meant that any time someone took a liberty with Micky, or threatened to do damage to his property, he made a call and it was sorted.

Sometimes, though, being under the protection of the Krays could backfire, and Charlie told me all about one time when it did. Micky had heard that some mug had threatened to trash his garage. I don't know why – maybe Micky had done or said something to upset him – but the guy should have known better. It was well known that Micky's car front was protected by the Krays.

The geezer was a loud mouth in a cheap suit, cussing

and snarling on the car front, when who should walk out of Micky's office but Ronnie Kray. His eyes narrowed, his fist clenched. The trouble maker didn't stand a chance. When Ron finished, he tossed the guy to the floor, and as he walked out of the garage he turned to one of Micky's employees and growled, 'Clear it up.' With that, he was gone.

The guy wasn't dead, but he wasn't far off. Micky panicked: 'You heard what Ron said.' They bundled the bleeding man into the back of one of the cars, then drove off in the direction of Victoria Park, hoping to find some bushes where they could dump the bloke.

They arrived at the park, but it was no good. There were too many people around. They had to think quickly. The guy was fading fast, and if they didn't do something then they'd end up with a corpse in the back of the car.

By now, night was falling, and Micky's employee was in a panic. He drove the car to the nearby Queen Mary hospital and sneaked in for a look. Good, the coast was clear. Amazingly, he managed to get the bloke into the hospital and dumped him on a trolley. He sunk his bloody hands deep into his overcoat pockets and walked towards the exit. And then he bumped straight into a nurse. She eyed him suspiciously. 'Can I help you?'

He shook his head. 'No, no thanks. I've just been visiting a friend. G'night.' And off he hurries.

The man pulled through. He never had evidence against Ron. And Ron being Ron gave the man a new lorry for his silence...

The Twins: Free at Last

Charlie wasn't involved personally in that incident, but as time went on he became more and more friendly with Ronnie and Reggie, and became an integral member of the firm. If Ron had sorted someone, they'd be banned from East London, and they knew that it was more than their life was worth come back until the twins said so. It was Charlie they'd have to call up to get that permission – Charlie would then speak to Ron and Reg and come back with a 'yes' or a 'no'. He was constantly by their side, one of their most trusted companions.

I asked Charlie what he thought made the twins so terrifying. He smiled, and said that one of the things he'd always remember them for was the absolute loyalty they felt towards each other. They would row all the time, of course, and often it resulted in a tear-up. But never in public. There was a strange link that existed between them because they were twins, and it meant that they were incredibly protective of each other. Ron never really liked Reg's wife Frances because she laid a claim to being almost as close to Reg as he was. In turn, Reg was unbelievably protective of Frances. Charlie recalls the time that Reg drove around all the clubs in London with Frances, saying to all of the doormen, 'If you ever let my wife into this club, I'll kill you.' He didn't want her anywhere near the scenes where Ron and he carried out their 'business'. When Frances committed suicide, Reg was absolutely devastated.

Charlie told me he'd never heard Ron ever raise his voice. I remembered Ron saying a similar thing to me: 'Kate, if you ask politely, you'll always get whatever you want.' Ron was a man who always appeared to be in complete control. His favourite tipple was dark brown ale, but nobody ever saw him drunk.

But everyone knew that the twins were more than capable of following through any threats of violence that they made. Charlie recalled an evening in the Double R, Ron and Reg's club. After a certain hour in the evening, they'd lock the doors from the inside – after that time if you were in, you were in, and if you were out, you were out. On this particular occasion, a group of half a dozen or so dockers were making a nuisance of themselves – big guys. They were boozed up, fuelled up and ready to go. Ron and Reg took them all on single-handed; Ron hit one so hard he flew into the air, slid along the floor and bashed straight into a juke box, jamming a record over and over again. The others ended up a mess on the floor.

Another time, they were in a restaurant with Oliver Reed the actor. Now Oliver Reed could be foul-mouthed. Reg and Ron were having a meal with some friends, and Oliver Reed was swearing and cussing in front of all the women who were there. Now if there was one thing Ron couldn't stand, it was a man acting disrespectfully in front of women. He didn't care if it was a famous actor or a dustman – he wouldn't have it. Ron put down his knife and fork. Reg knew what was going to happen. Ron apologised to the ladies. Oliver Reed was laughing and drinking as Ron approached him. He was a big man. He stood up, and Ron upped him. Oliver hit the floor with a thud.

Reg and Ron had morals. A code of honour that never changed. If they got the needle with anyone – even a famous actor – then they sorted it. Charlie told me how

The Twins: Free at Last

after Ron shot George Cornell, he went round all the pubs telling everybody, 'It was me. I shot Cornell.' Charlie, along with many others, had no time for Cornell. I asked him what he was like, and he gave me all the details. Cornell was in a gang called the Watley Street Gang. They were out of Stepney, and were a right rough bunch. Cornell made his first mistake when he went on to Ron and Reg's patch and done a geezer with an axe. After that he defected to South of the river and joined the Richardsons. Ron knew at that point it was either him or Cornell – the rest is history.

One of Charlie's jobs towards the end of the Sixties was to look after John Pearson. He was the writer that wrote the bestselling book *The Profession of Violence*. It was the first book ever written about the twins; it was in their heyday, at the height of their professional career.

The very fact that somebody wanted to write a book about them really pleased Ron and Reg. It would turn them into instant celebrities, and they loved it. They let Pearson shadow them around everywhere, and it was Charlie's job to drive them round all the clubs. But Ron didn't really like Pearson. He needed a place to stay, so Ron put him up in 'The Dungeon', a dingy little basement opposite the house in Vallance Road. After a while, Ron got so sick of Pearson that he upped him, and when the book was finally published, the twins hated what he had written. That aside, though, the twins did get a twice yearly pension from that book right up until their death.

Charlie was with the twins right up to the very end. In fact,

The Final Night of Freedom

he was with them on their very last night of freedom. He told me the whole story after Reg's death.

The twins were entertaining in the Astor club, one of their haunts off Berkley Square in Mayfair. Their guests were two very important people – the Kaufman brothers from New York who were the twins' immediate links with the Mafia in America. Ron and Reg wanted to put on a show for them.

In a nearby bar, a great band were playing. The twins decided that it would be good to have the band at the Astor club so that they could put on some entertainment for the Kaufmans. They used their 'influence' to hijack the band and move them over to their club.

Part of the entourage that night were two black dancers – the Clarke brothers. Ron went up to them and said, 'When the band play, you fucking dance, alright?' Which is just what they did. The band kicked in, the Clarke brothers started dancing. Half and hour passed; an hour. The dancers were getting tired, but Ron's steely gaze encouraged them to continue...

Two hours passed. The Clarke brothers were exhausted. One of them went up to Ronnie and panted, 'Ron, we can't dance no more.'

'What do you mean, you can't dance no more? You're fucking dancers, aren't you? Dance! And make sure you're smiling while you do it!'

'But Ron...' Something in the look Ron gave him told him that it wasn't a good time to argue. The brothers took to the dance floor once again, and started dancing with as much energy as they could, hips shaking, legs moving, arms in the air. It didn't take long for them to collapse completely.

The next morning Charlie was back home in bed. The phone rang. He peered at his alarm clock and saw that it was seven o'clock in the morning. He rubbed his eyes.

'The twins have been nicked.'

At first he didn't understand what the caller was saying, but he was startled by the urgency in the guy's voice.

'Who the fuck's talking?'

'Charlie, it's me. Checa Berry. The twins have been nicked. It's serious. Get dressed. I'll be around in ten minutes.'

Checa explained that there had been a dawn raid and that Reg and Ron had been nicked. Charlie was amazed – it had only been a couple of hours ago that they'd been mob-handed in the Astor club having a good old knees up and watching the Clarke brothers bop till they dropped. Charlie had given Ron a lift home at about six in the morning and dropped him at Braithwaite House where he had a flat. Even at the time he'd noticed a heavy police presence all round the East End.

'Something's going down,' he'd said to Ron. 'Maybe I should drive around the back roads.'

But Ron was on a real high. 'Fuck 'em,' he laughed. 'They're all mugs.'

Everyone roared with laughter. I wonder if they would have laughed so much if they'd realised that that night was to be the twins' last night of freedom...

The Final Night of Freedom

I asked Charlie how he felt now that the twins had died. His words were so moving that they speak for themselves:

I'm glad Ron didn't die in Broadmoor. And as for Reg, he should have been let out years ago. But at least they let him out to die. At least they were both spared the indignity of dying in prison.

Broadmoor's gone mad since Ron's been gone. Peter Sutcliffe, the Yorkshire Ripper, has been blinded in one eye. Ian Kay, another inmate, stabbed him in both eyes with a felt-tipped pen. Sutcliffe was on the same ward as Ron, in the very next cell. The stabbing would never have happened if Ron was still there; he just wouldn't have allowed it. Sutcliffe wants a glass eye but Broadmoor has refused on the grounds that he could smash it up and use all the little bits of glass to cut his own wrists or cut someone else. Sounds crazy, but plausible, given the nut-cases that are there.

I don't wish Ronnie back in Broadmoor, not for one minute. There is nothing I would have loved more than to see him back in the East End having a drink with his friends.

For me, when Ronnie and Reggie died, it was the end of an era. The end of the Swinging Sixties. End of the gangsters. End of the good life. My Life. It's just not the same any more. When the twins died, a big part of me died with them.

REG ON PRISON

*P*rison life is not glamourous and believe me I know.
Real life goes on without you on the other side of
the high walls. I like to think that I will be a good,
rather than bad, influence to those youngsters who face the
loss of freedom.

THE MANAGING
DIRECTORS OF
BRITISH CRIME

Just because the twins were inside, it didn't mean they couldn't go on with business. Ron and Reg were the best money-getters I've ever met. That's all they thought of while they were inside. They were like hamsters on a tread wheel chasing money – getting a pile, giving it away, then back on the wheel.

Even after they were convicted, they continued to run their empire like the businessmen that they were. Whilst they were still alive, I had to keep quiet about their activities, but I know that they would each be earning at least £100,000 a year for the last thirty years.

I did many things for Ron. I didn't mind, that was all part of being married. Late one evening, I got a phonecall asking me to visit him urgently. I drove to Broadmoor at the crack of dawn trying to avoid the rush-hour traffic. Ron was on good form.

'You look happy,' I said.

He was in no mood for idle chat.

'Never mind all that,' he said. 'I want you to go to Waterlooville in Hampshire.'

He was happy, so I knew it was to do with money. Nothing made Ron happier than when he had a nice few quid coming.

'I want you to pick up £85,000.' He laughed.

My jaw dropped open. I could have tucked my chin in my knickers.

'Eighty-five grand!' I couldn't believe it.

'Yeah, in notes,' he purred.

I was used to picking up large amounts of cash for Ron, but this was an unusually large amount, even for him. I didn't know what it was for, or where it came from. I didn't ask. Ron didn't explain; he just gave me a long list of names where he wanted the cash to go.

On this occasion, he decided that he would send someone with me to ride shotgun. I can't remember who he was, all I can remember is he was big and mean.

Ron insisted that I follow his instructions to the letter. I travelled to Hampshire, wondering if it was going to be a wasted journey. Eighty-five grand was a lot of money. I couldn't help thinking to myself that it must have been some blag for Ron's cut to be that big.

I did hope nothing would go wrong. There had been the odd occasion when I'd been to collect money for him, and when I'd got there something had gone wrong or someone had been nicked. Whatever the reason, the money wasn't there and, oh boy, did Ron get the needle.

It was a long journey to Waterlooville, and I just hoped this was not going to be a wasted trip although Ron seemed very confident.

I parked my car in the small car park at the rear of the bank. As I walked into the bank shadowed by my minder, I was humming the song 'Me and My Shadow' under my breath. We must have looked a right pair! The bank was full. We queued. I gave the cashier all the relevant paperwork. The young girl behind the counter looked at me and then at my shadow.

'Wait here, Mrs Kray,' she said gingerly.

She went to the Manager's office. I dread to think what she said. His door opened — he stuck his head out. He looked at me, then at my shadow, and shut the door again. The door opened for a second time. The cashier and the Manager came out of the office together.

They mumbled to each other, looked at me, then mumbled again. I looked around the bank trying to appear inconspicuous. The more I tried to look innocent, the more guilty I felt. At that point, it did cross my mind to wonder exactly where the money was coming from. But then I thought, if the money isn't kosher, Ron would never allow me to go and get it. The Manager broke my thoughts.

'Mrs Kray.'

My heart leapt into my mouth.

'How would you like the money?' he said.

I stuttered. 'Er … Er … Large notes, please.'

It took the cashier and the Manager ages to count the money in front of me. I couldn't wait to get out of that

The Twins: Free at Last

bank. I got back into my car and drove out of Waterlooville.

A few miles up the small country lane, I pulled the car over into a lay-by. I opened a can of coke and took a large gulp. It should have been something stronger — sometimes it's a pity I don't drink alcohol. I offered the can to my minder. He shook his head, turning his nose up.

'Let's have a sort out,' he urged.

I pulled the money bag out from the glove compartment and banged it down on the dashboard. It was a huge bag. I peered inside. It stunk. Slowly, I started to count the money into small piles. One hundred. Two hundred. Three hundred. When the piles were complete, I stuck a coloured 'post-it' note on the top with the name of each person who was going to receive the cash.

It took ages to sort out £85,000. But who's complaining? I kept looking at my watch. I knew Ron would be wondering if things had gone smoothly.

My instructions were that once I had got the cash and counted it out into bundles, I had to visit Ron. I didn't want to be late, as I knew he would be wondering if things were all right. That was probably my own doing because I had teased him previously saying that once I had got the cash I was going to run off and send him a postcard from a sunny desert island.

I laughed. So did he. Thank God.

I dashed up the M3 to reach Ron for the afternoon visit. I just made the visiting hall by 2.30pm. Eagerly, Ron was waiting. I walked into the hall. He stood up and looked at me trying to gauge my expression. I raised my eyes to the heavens, shook my head and threw my hands in the air in defeat. He looked angry and pissed off. I realised it was not the best time to have a joke with him.

I smiled, winked and rubbed my hands together.

'You little minx,' he laughed. 'You got it, ain't ya?'

'Of course I got it,' I replied. He hugged me tight.

'Where the fuck is it?'

'In the glove compartment of my car, that's where.'

'But ... but ... you can't ...' he spluttered.

With my hand held high, I stopped him in his tracks, like a policeman holding up the traffic. 'It's all right. Calm down. It's being baby-sat by the fucking shadow.'

'That's all right then.' That seemed to pacify him.

We spent the whole visit sorting out the money. I spent the entire next day being Father Christmas distributing it. Ron eventually got round to telling me where the £85,000 came from.

It was legit. It was paid to Ron from the Fugitive film company as proceeds from the hit film *The Krays*, starring the Kemp brothers from the pop group Spandau Ballet. £85,000 was the first payment — more was due but, unfortunately for Reg and Ron, the company went bust.

I was astonished at the amount of money that flowed into the Kray coffers, even though the two key players were locked away for 30 years. For five years I was drawn into the network doing cash drops and making pay-outs to friends for services rendered. I had one mission in life at that time — to help make Ronnie's life inside as comfortable as possible.

I was amazed that the authorities did not seem to realise Ronnie was operating his rackets inside Broadmoor.

The Twins: Free at Last

It was done under their noses. I suppose they didn't realise what was going on. I'm glad, because that was what kept Ron going. He would try any business venture, no matter how far-fetched, in order to make money. He was the best money-getter I have ever met or am ever likely to meet. He was a tough businessman, but fair. There weren't any villains whom Ron didn't know. His black address book was the *Who's Who* of the underworld. I automatically assumed that all the gangsters knew each other. Not true. They all knew Ron, but not each other.

All the gangsters looked up to Ronnie while he was in Broadmoor, and treated him with the utmost respect.

I saw tens of thousands pour in to Ron's coffers week after week … and pour out again. Of course, none of it went directly to him in Broadmoor, but everything he wanted was paid for out of his cut and was brought in for him.

The bulk of Ron's money never passed through Broadmoor and, for years, I became Ron's trusted confidante. I dealt with his money. I had his account books. He trusted me to get cash out for him to take it here, take it there, pay so and so, pick something up for someone. I never really knew what all the transactions were about.

Some of the names Ronnie used were coded, and it was obvious they weren't straight dealings. I didn't want to know. If I didn't know anything then I couldn't say anything. I knew I was becoming drawn into dangerous territory, but I suppose that was one of his attractions. Ron was a very exciting man.

Once I had completed a drop, I normally didn't see

Ron until the next day but I always rung him at 8.00pm every single evening.

We used a code to communicate because Ron was not allowed to use the telephone then, so I spoke to the nurses. I used to ring up and ask if Ron was OK. Ron would always stand outside the small office on the ward waiting for my call.

I was never late ringing him. It didn't matter where I was in the world, I would make sure Ron got his call at 8.00pm. I didn't say much. I would just ask if he was all right. The voice on the end of the line would say, 'Yes, he's OK. Just fine.'

Ron would know it was me. He would put his head round the door and ask if I had picked his suit up from the cleaners. The screw would relay the message and by the tone of the voice I realised they considered it trivial. If only they realised the importance of the message. If I replied yes, I had picked up his suit, I would hear them call out to Ron.

'Yes, Ron, she has picked up your suit.'

He would call back, 'Oh good. Tell her I said goodnight and God bless.' He would walk away with a smile on his face, confident of the fact that everything had gone smoothly.

On the other hand, if I said that I hadn't picked up his suit from the cleaners, he would still say 'goodnight and God bless', but walk away cursing.

Reg was just the same. Like Ron he was a like a little hamster on a wheel, scurrying away, chasing money all the time. People would come to him with most weird ideas you've ever heard: 'Reg, I've got this bloke says he can turn water into petrol.' Great idea, give him ten grand. Sometimes it came off, sometimes it didn't. Whatever happened, they could always get their hands on money when they needed it.

But as soon as they had money, they spent it. I had to send £5,000 once to an address. Later I discovered that it was to find someone who'd been sprung from Broadmoor. At the time, I didn't know what the money was for: 'Don't ask questions,' said Ron, 'just do it.' Other times they would spend it on more worthy causes. Ron would see something in the paper, some kid who need help or something, and say to me, 'Send four grand to that.'

'But Ron, you've only got four grand left.'

'Don't matter, just send it. I'll get some more.'

And they always did...

RON ON MADNESS

I'm a chronic paranoid schizophrenic. Even the experts are not sure what causes it – or what cures it, if anything. But I know when I'm not feeling well. And I know what medication I need: I take Largactil and Stemetil to calm my nerves. On top of that I take Dispipal to counteract the side effects of the Stemetil – often people suffer from loss of muscle control which means they make involuntary movements. I also have a Modecate injection once a fortnight.

In layman's terms I can only describe it as a 'radio' on in my head. I strain to listen to what the radio is telling *me. Normally it's telling me to hurt or kill someone. My medication helps but it turns down the 'radio' and I have to strain to hear it.*

LIFE AND DEATH
IN BROADMOOR

*'Sometimes, Kate, I think
it would have been kinder to hang me...'*

Ronnie Kray

Broadmoor is a dangerous place; a home to dangerous men. I found this out when an obsessed nutter started stalking me. His name was Frank Butler. A name I'll never forget. If it wasn't for the good advice of Reggie Kray, I might not have been telling this story today...

Ron had given Butler's wife my name, address and phone number for some reason, and Butler was soon to be released from Broadmoor after serving 18 years. It was Christmas 1990. My phone kept ringing morning, noon and

The Twins: Free at Last

night. Every time I picked it up, it was the same person — Butler. He sounded odd — it wasn't his Geordie accent, but he would say strange things. At first he just paid me veiled compliments, like how he liked me and how lucky Ron was to have me as his wife. Then he started to get a little more serious, drooling, and wondering why didn't I let him take care of me sexually because Ron was in prison and he was out.

Then he blatantly asked if he could have sex with me. I got really angry. How dare he take such a liberty? I snapped at him, 'Don't you dare talk to me like that otherwise I will tell Ron.'

From that moment his mood changed. Things turned ugly. The phone calls were no longer polite — they were filth. He said that he would cut the tendons in the back of my legs if I didn't have sex with him. The phone calls carried on for three days. Day and night the phone never stopped ringing. It was starting to drive me crazy. Every time I picked the phone up, it was him. In one day alone he had rung 32 times. I was at the end of my tether.

The phone rang again. I snatched it off the hook and screamed, 'Leave me alone.'

This time it was Reggie on the phone. 'What is the matter with you, Kate?' he asked. I told him all about the filthy phone calls and asked him to phone the filthy pervert to tell him to leave me alone.

Reg pointed out, 'It would do no good me phoning him, because he knows you are married to Ron and that didn't stop him making the calls in the first place. Don't take any chances. He is obviously a nutter. Phone

Life and Death in Broadmoor

Broadmoor and tell them what is going on and then phone the police immediately.'

For Reggie to tell me to phone the police, I realised it must be extremely serious. I rang Broadmoor and told them what was happening. They told me to go straight to the police. The urgency in their voice convinced me to act fast, so I went straight to the police station in Maidstone. I felt embarrassed telling them that I was Ronnie Kray's wife and that a nutter was after me. They were very sympathetic and took some notes. I thought a visit from the Old Bill would be enough to stop him, but I soon found out just how wrong I was.

By the time I got home, I couldn't believe it. There were Old Bill everywhere. I pulled my car up outside my house and a burly policewoman ushered me inside. She told me that they had spoken to Broadmoor and they said that Frank Butler was one of the most dangerous men they had ever held there. The police insisted that I go to a safe house. I thought they were going over the top a bit, but I suppose they knew best. Pressure pads were installed under the carpets in my home just in case he managed to get in.

DI Pat Geary, the officer in charge of the case, stayed in my house and pretended that she was me. Butler was obviously mentally ill. But he still kept ringing. I was glad that he was talking to the policewoman and not to me. He even threatened to kill her, still thinking that it was me. The police in Newcastle-upon-Tyne, his home town, were notified, but Butler was nowhere to be found.

Everyone was concerned. It was a waiting game. They all knew it was only a matter of time before he

The Twins: Free at Last

surfaced. They didn't have to wait long. It was the following day when the police picked him up in Maidstone town centre. He had come all the way from Newcastle-upon-Tyne to kill me.

To look at him, you would think that butter wouldn't melt in his mouth. He didn't have horns sticking out of the top of his head or 'rapist' tattooed on his forehead. That was the trouble — he just looked normal, or as normal as can be for a 65-year-old wearing a cheap wig. Pat Geary made me laugh when she said he looked more like an old granddad rather than an evil rapist. She said that when they were interviewing him, he was really placid and softly spoken. But when they went to take his wig off to photograph him, he went mad, shouting and screaming at the officers. She said he was like a wild man.

I did laugh when she said that but, in reality, it was not funny. Neither was his criminal record. It turned out that his record was as long as your arm, starting way back in 1945. He had a history of indecently assaulting women and young girls. Indeed, he was sentenced to 18 years in Broadmoor for cutting the tendons in the back of a young girl's legs — exactly what he had threatened to do to me. After his arrest, I went up to visit Ron and he said, 'Frank Butler is a dangerous man, so when it goes to court you must attend to give evidence.' He explained that if I refused and he went on to hurt somebody else — someone not as strong as me — I would never forgive myself. Of course, he was right.

When the day came to go to court, I went. The charge was threatening to murder. I agreed that he should

Life and Death in Broadmoor

be let off with a caution because, while on bail, he had stabbed somebody and the police wanted the higher charge of attempted murder. I hope he is still away somewhere and remains there indefinitely. But I don't think he ever went back to Broadmoor because, if Ron could have got to him, he would have killed him – no doubt.

25 July 1979. The twins had been banged up for ten years. Ron wasn't well. He was in Parkhurst, and nobody could control him. He ended up in a punishment block, naked, a small blanket and a radio for comfort. And then he heard the voice of a screw coming through the door. 'You're being nutted off, Ron. How d'you like that?'

Nutted off. He knew what that meant. They were sending him to Broadmoor.

Ron had been in Broadmoor before. The first time he was there was back in 1963, when he went to visit his friend, Roy 'Pretty Boy' Shaw. 'What's it like in here, Roy?' he asked him.

'Well,' said Roy, 'it's alright, apart from it's full of poofs.'

'Oh,' smiled Ron, 'is it? Smashin'!'

Now he was going to find out what Broadmoor was like for himself. Ron never said a word. He didn't give a damn. He knew they couldn't hurt him anymore. Three whole months they had kept him in solitary confinement. Three months. It must have seemed like three years. A weaker person would have gone mad being kept in solitary that long. Ron was already suffering from a mental problem. Three months of being kept in the dark, alone and naked,

The Twins: Free at Last

in what they called the 'strongbox', tipped him over the edge. The strongbox was a room, a square room. The whole thing was made of concrete, with a little bed in the middle. It wasn't really a bed, just a slab of cold stone.

The only person to show Ron any compassion or kindness was a medical officer called David Cooper. He gave him the small transistor radio and allowed him to keep it in the strongbox.

After that living hell, it's a wonder Ron was alive. He later told me that when he was eventually transferred to Broadmoor, he was the maddest he had ever been in his entire life.

The journey from Parkhurst to Broadmoor was a long one. Ron remembered it well. He said it was a bright sunny day. He was handcuffed and shoved into the back of a white prison van. Five screws sat in the back with him. The van boarded the ferry from Ryde to Portsmouth. Ron took a deep breath and held it. The air was different. Fresher. Seagulls squawked. The noise was deafening. The screws laughed and joked all the way. Ron said nothing. The van pulled off the ferry and down the motorway to Crowthorne, Berkshire.

Ron peered out of the small window on the side of the van. It was a hot afternoon in July. People were out in their cars, some were towing caravans, they looked happy. Deep inside, Ron envied them. The van pulled off the motorway into what seemed like a big park. The guards started moving about inside the van. Ron looked out of the small window again and saw a big sign on a white board: 'Broadmoor Special Hospital. Private Property.'

Life and Death in Broadmoor

The van laboured as it climbed the steep hill towards the hospital The sun flickered through the tree-lined drive and Ron caught a glimpse of the hospital for the first time. It was a big, imposing Victorian building. It looked every bit an asylum.

Ron was amazed that the bricks were orange — bright orange. The walls were high. The huge wooden gates opened and swallowed the prison van.

Once inside the small courtyard, Ron was struck by the silence. He expected to see patients, doctors and nurses, the hustle and bustle of a hospital. But there was nothing — just silence.

He was taken directly to the admission ward. There he was stripped, searched internally and bathed in the compulsory six inches of water.

He never said a word as they shaved his head and covered him in a foul smelling lice powder. He was given a white paper boiler suit to wear and was escorted into a cell where the door slammed and bolted behind him. He slumped down on the small bed and pulled the itchy grey blanket over his shoulders.

During those early weeks and months he was seen by an endless stream of doctors, psychologists, education officers and social workers and was assessed by them all. Finally, he was placed on the appropriate medication. Four times a day he took Stemetol capsules to quieten his nerves. He was given Disipal for the side-effects caused by the Stemetol, which sometimes made his limbs shake. Every fortnight, he had an injection of Modicate, which is a drug specifically to curb the symptoms of schizophrenia. It took three months for his condition to be brought under control.

Eventually, he was well enough to be transferred on to a ward in the mainstream hospital. All the wards in Broadmoor are named after towns and counties in England: Taunton, Kent, Suffolk. Ron was taken to Somerset House.

Ron settled down on the ward quickly. However, the daily routine was hard for him to get used to at first. Every day was the same. Unlock at 7.00am. Slop out. Wash and shave, then wait in line while the razors are counted. They can't take any chances in case the patients have suicidal tendencies or, even worse, attempt to kill again.

That was the main event of the day. After that, they were taken to the day-room where they sat until 9.00pm unless they had a visit. In the day-room, there were five rows of chairs across the room, and a television set at the end, which was constantly blaring. Down the side of the room was a line of blue chairs. These were for the staff. They watched the patients' every move and listened to every conversation. Ron stayed on Somerset Ward for the next 12 years, leaving the ward only for visits and the occasional hospital check-up.

Ron didn't mind. One thing is for sure, he was better off there and considered himself luckier than when he was in Parkhurst. He was allowed more visits in Broadmoor than when he was in prison. In fact, he could have two visits a day if he wanted. In Parkhurst, he was allowed only two visits a month. Also, he could wear his own clothes in Broadmoor. The food was better, too. But there was a down side.

Norfolk House was the punishment block at

Life and Death in Broadmoor

Broadmoor. Its name would strike fear into anyone who had been unlucky enough to be detained there. At first, Ron was reluctant to talk about his experience on Norfolk House. His face tightened and he scowled.

'Nothing in this world can compare to the punishment block in Broadmoor,' he whispered.

I was shocked. I imagined that prison would be tougher. Ron shook his head.

'Norfolk House is your worst nightmare come true.'

The look on Ron's face said it all. I was intrigued.

'Why is it a nightmare, Ron?' I asked.

He lowered his eyes. It was as if he was too embarrassed to tell me. Gently, I rubbed his back to reassure him.

'Tell me, Ron. Nothing can be that bad.'

He took the last drag of his cigarette and slowly stubbed it out in the ash tray. He turned his head to the side and exhaled the smoke and sighed.

'OK, if you want to know then I'll tell you.'

I watched him carefully as he started to talk.

'I'd got into an argument with another patient. I can't remember what about. I got mad. Bloody mad. I hit him. The punch broke his jaw. Alarm bells were sounded.

'Before I knew it, I was bundled to the ground by five or six burly officers. I kicked, punched and bit every fucking one of the dirty bastards. But I didn't stand a chance.

'They dragged me along the corridor by my legs. They didn't walk, they ran with me. Everyone that was standing in the corridor got out of the way. The officers tried to drag me into a cell but I held on to the door-frame. Three of them tugged at my legs. They pulled so hard that my trousers came down around my knees. I held on to that fucking door-frame for dear life. One of the dirty bastards kicked my hands. Still I wouldn't let go. He got annoyed and bent my fingers so far back I thought they would snap. I screamed out in agony and let go of the door-frame. The three officers that were pulling my legs fell backwards. The cell door slammed shut. Five of the fuckers grabbed me. I tried to fight them off. I didn't stand a chance. They threw me on to a bed. Well, I say a bed it was more like an examination table. It had thick leather straps at the side with big shiny buckles. I struggled like fuck but they overpowered me and strapped my arms to the side of the table. Next, my legs were buckled in place.

'I couldn't move. The officers were worn out wrestling with me. They slumped against the wall to catch their breath.

'I wriggled and wriggled, pulling at the straps. They laughed.

'"You ain't going nowhere, Ron."'

'I spat at them and cursed them. But they wouldn't stop laughing. The cell door swung open. In walked a doctor. He said, "Remove his clothes."

'The dirty bastards took my clothes off so I was naked.'

For a moment, Ron paused. I looked at him. He was angry, upset. He poured his chilled lager and lit another fag.

'You don't have to tell me any more if you don't

Life and Death in Broadmoor

want to,' I said.

He shook his head. 'You wanted to know so I'll tell you. The doctor turned to a small trolley that was directly behind him and pulled on a pair of surgical gloves. He didn't look at me. Again, I tugged at the straps. The doctor motioned to the officers.

'"Hold him still."

'He approached me holding a syringe. A screw held the top of my arm. I tried to bite him. Someone grabbed my head. The doctor flicked the syringe. Small droplets of a clear liquid exploded from the end of the needle. He plunged the syringe into my arm. I closed my eyes tight and held my breath. I felt the cold fluid run through my veins. My heart started to pound like a drum. I felt dizzy, sick.

'I tried to fight the effect of the drug, but it was no good. The screws that were holding me let go. I clenched my fists and pulled at the leather straps that were holding me down. My back arched and I went into a convulsion.

'What happened to me over the next five months is vague. I still have flashbacks. I must have been going in and out of consciousness. I remember terrible hallucinations. My most vivid recollections are of devils and demons screeching and screaming at me.

'Watching the ceiling getting closer and closer to my face, the fear of being trapped in that room for ever was probably the most fearsome experience of my entire life. Colours, those bright flashing colours so bright they stabbed my eyes whether opened or closed — it made no difference. I felt fear, uncontrollable fear like I've never felt before. Loneliness. I don't remember being unstrapped the

45

whole time I was in that room, but I do remember the nurses giving me more mind-blowing drugs.

I looked at Ron. Remembering it all made his face almost screw up in pain. He sipped at his drink. He looked tired.

'I never want to go back to Norfolk,' he whispered. 'Sometimes, in my head, I can still hear the cries of other patients. They used to scream.'

I didn't know what to say. I just looked at him and those sad eyes. There was a silence. Neither of us said anything for a minute or two.

Five months they kept Ron on Norfolk — the House of Correction, the staff call it. Five long months. He must have gone to hell and back. It was a nightmare, one that was to haunt him for the rest of his life. I suppose that's why there used to be little or no trouble in Broadmoor. The threat of Norfolk must have loomed over every inmate.

Ron often talked about Broadmoor. He already knew a lot about the place long before he was transferred there. It was way back in 1963 when Ron first went there. That time it was to visit Roy Shaw. Roy told Ron that it wasn't a bad place to do bird. It was ironic that he ended up there later.

Another friend of Ron's called Nobby Clark pre-warned Ron, saying that Broadmoor could be heaven or hell, it just depended on you. He should know. Nobby did his time the hard way. Nobby was a wiry old goat. He had long grey hair and a long grey beard with bright twinkling eyes. He had a troubled life and was one crazy bastard. While he was serving time in Parkhurst, he speared another inmate, stabbing him while he was lying in the bath.

He was transferred to Broadmoor and was never released. He had a heart-attack and died there. Ron told me the story of Nobby several times. He never forgot his warning that it could be heaven or hell.

In the first few years of Ron's time in Broadmoor, he wanted to find out all about the place. He got a book out of the hospital library. It was out of date but that didn't matter to Ron. The book was written in the early 1950s by a man called Ralph Partridge. It was called Broadmoor: *A History of Criminal Lunacy and Its Problems*.

It didn't paint a true picture of how Broadmoor is today, but it was a starting point. It had photographs and conversations with older patients and staff at the hospital. In the early days it was barbaric. The patients were kept like animals.

This intrigued Ron enough to encourage him to find out more about the asylum. Broadmoor was built by a man called Joshua Jebb. He must have been a latter-day builder — a Victorian Mr Barratt. It was originally built because of a madman with a gun who had tried to kill the King of England. They had nowhere to put him. They said he was totally mad. He had to be to try to kill the King. But what to do with him? Make an example of him. But how? The answer was to build an asylum for him so he could spend the rest of his miserable life there — hence Broadmoor. By a strange twist of fate, the King later became mad himself.

Crowthorne in Berkshire was chosen because, in those days, it was thought that the fresh air would be therapeutic for the lunatics. As if a raving nutter would care

The Twins: Free at Last

less what the air was like. Boredom is the biggest enemy in Broadmoor. The patients just have so much time to kill, if you pardon the pun.

If you aren't paranoid when you go into Broadmoor, you soon will be. The staff watch your every move. Observation by nursing staff is a key factor in the security. It has to be. The patients are, after all, the most dangerous in Britain. Certain patients are 'grasses' and feed the staff with information thinking that it will win them favour. It's just tittle-tattle really, nothing of any importance. It's not as if they are informing on some elaborate escape plan.

It is rare that anyone escapes from inside Broadmoor. Most escapes occur while patients are on outside work parties. All movement throughout the hospital, by patients and staff, is watched closely.

The whole hospital is saturated with video cameras which are linked to a central control room.

Staff always know where every patient is, at any time of the day or night. If they need to check out an individual, it's easy — they hunt them down with the camera. Forget some program on TV – this really is Big Brother.

The walls around Broadmoor are the highest around any prison in Europe, higher than the Berlin Wall used to be. The wall is designed to have a psychological effect on the inmates. At its lowest point it is 30ft high. If you had thoughts of clambering over it, you might just as well forget it, unless you're Superman.

Just to make doubly sure, the wall has an infra-red beam running the length of it as a further security measure.

Life and Death in Broadmoor

The beam is so sensitive it can be broken by the smallest creature, setting off an immediate alert in the control tower. Officers with dogs patrol the perimeter constantly. When the alarm is sounded, the whole hospital grinds to a halt. The patients are head-counted back to their cells until the panic is over. It happens often. If someone is missing, the hospital goes on red alert. The siren is sounded to warn the surrounding area. Mothers gather up their children in case it's not a false alarm, hoping and praying that it's not a child murderer on the loose. A photograph of the escapee is faxed to all the police stations in the area. Road-blocks are set up within a 15-mile radius. Broadmoor is like Nazi concentration camp. It has to be.

All Broadmoor patients are suffering from psychotic disorders, many are schizophrenics. Most schizophrenics have ancestors or relations with mental disorders. In Ron's case, his mental problems can be traced back to his great-grandfather, Critcha Lee, who was a gypsy and cattle-dealer from Bermondsey and died in Claybury Madhouse. Ron's grandfather's brother, who was called Jewy, also died there. Ron was a paranoid schizophrenic. He struggled with the illness for many, many years — maybe for most of his life.

On one of our visits, I asked Ron to describe what schizophrenia was and, more importantly, how it felt. It was rare that Ron would talk about his illness. But this particular day he felt good and explained in great detail.

What he said shocked me — it must have been a battle which he had to fight every day. He said that it was the voices in his head that drove him mad. He described it vividly. It was like having a radio on in his mind, like

The Twins: Free at Last

background music never going away, a continuous noise he couldn't turn off. But, instead of listening to his favourite song, the radio in his head whispered evil things: 'He's going to kill you, kill him first.'

The voices never stopped. The drugs helped a bit but, he said, they just seemed to turn the radio down, so he strained to hear the voices. He then had to concentrate really hard just to catch what the voices were saying. He said that he could be on a visit or talking to someone on the ward, but he never heard a word they said. He was too busy listening to the evil voices.

It was a constant struggle to decide what was reality and what was not — what was evil and what was good.

When Ron was feeling like that, more often than not he would cancel his visits. He did this for two reasons. One, he didn't want anyone to see him like that; and two, he didn't want to distrust his friends. He explained to me early on in our relationship that, from time to time, he may not want to see me or anyone else. I got used to his ways just like any normal married couple. After a while, I began to see the signs myself when Ron was 'going into one' as he put it. I could tell straight away. It was his eyes. They were sort of blank. Empty. Dead.

Ron knew himself when he wasn't feeling right. He would see the doctor and ask him to increase or decrease his medication. The drugs helped the bad dreams and the depression, but what nothing could cure was the terrible feeling of loneliness. When Ron felt like that, it was best just to leave him alone. That's the way he preferred it.

Usually in prisons, grasses and sex offenders are

Life and Death in Broadmoor

segregated. In Broadmoor it doesn't happen like that. Ron said that if he was to slap every nonce (sex offender) he came across in Broadmoor, then he would be slapping someone every five minutes. Everyone in Broadmoor has committed a horrendous crime, but the difference there is that the offender is suffering from some sort of psychological disorder. Ron hated sex offenders and child killers and hated mixing with them, but he had no choice. Even so, he soon let it be known that such beasts should stay away from him and they got the message.

In the autumn of 1990, things changed for the better in Ron's life. He was going to move from the old Somerset House block that had been his home for 12 years to a brand-new block called Oxford House. Ron was told he would be on Henley Ward, on the first floor.

He was glad and had been looking forward to the move for months. In Somerset House he had to slop out every morning as he didn't have his own toilet. All the toilets and washing facilities were at the end of the corridor, four sinks for thirty patients. The toilets had no privacy; neither did their cells. In the new block, all the cells had a toilet and wash basin. They even had a built-in wardrobe.

But the biggest thing that pleased Ron was the window. For the first time in nearly 25 years, there were no bars on the windows because the glass is unbreakable.

Every year, a patient is entitled to a tribunal and every three years it is compulsory that the patient attends. Ron considered these a waste of time. I wanted to attend them but he told me not to bother because there was no way they were going to release him. A tribunal is made up

The Twins: Free at Last

of a judge, a doctor and a member of the public.

Very few patients are discharged by a tribunal. The only way out of section 65 is to convince the psychiatrist looking after you that you are fit to be discharged. He then has to persuade the Home Secretary. No Home Secretary in his right mind was going to put his political career on the line by agreeing to release Ron.

On one particular occasion, he had had a boring morning. He was fed up. It was dinnertime. The patients filed in to get their meals. Ron sat down at the table. It was just another day, the same as all the rest. No one spoke. They were only interested in their food. All of a sudden, one of the elderly patients stood up, pulled his trousers and pants down to his ankles and, at the top of his voice, yelled, 'Fuck my arse.'

Nobody stopped eating. Nobody looked up. A nurse who was sitting chatting in the corner put his teacup down, sighed and tutted.

'Come on, pull your trousers up.'

The old patient was adamant. 'It was you,' he pointed at the nurse. 'You're God and it was you that fucked me up the arse last night.'

The nurse shook his head. 'Yeah. That's right. It was lovely. Now eat your fucking dinner.'

The old boy pulled his trousers up, sat down, and continued to eat his dinner. Just another day in the loony bin.

Ronnie Kray didn't exactly like being locked away in Broadmoor, but he made sure life was as enjoyable and comfortable as possible under the circumstances. He didn't really have a champagne and caviar lifestyle, but it wasn't far from that. Just his name, his charisma and an abundance of cash always ensured that he got what he wanted, when he wanted.

Ron never had to threaten anybody. He always told me, 'Speak nicely to people and they always do what you want.' He must have been right because he had a network of 'helpers' inside Broadmoor, fellow inmates, ready, some even anxious, to get close to him.

I don't know if it was his name that did it or the reflected glory of being his 'friend', which perhaps gave them a greater status inside. Then again, maybe it was all the presents he bought them. But one thing is for sure; everybody seemed to want to be around Ron, helping and doing things for him. I suppose it was their claim to fame.

For instance, Ronnie never washed or ironed his shirts, or even pressed his trousers. He always got someone else to do it for him. There was always a little band of 'helpers' or 'yes men' as I called them. I had visions of all these nutters running about saying, 'Yes, Ron ... no, Ron ... three bags full, Ron ...'

Charlie was the inmate who use to wash, starch and iron Ron's shirts. He was given a jar of coffee every week. Ron's shirts were his speciality. He took great pride in making sure that they were just how Ron liked them. Ron changed his shirt after every visit, making 14 shirts a week. Charlie did them week in, week out, for years, for just a jar of coffee a week.

Long before Ron and I were married, I decided that

The Twins: Free at Last

I would do my bit to try to make Ron's life as happy and comfortable as I possibly could in Broadmoor, even if that meant putting my own liberty at risk. It was not difficult to get Ronnie the five-star treatment, and one of the treats I organised was a seafood banquet whenever Reggie came to visit him.

Ron always liked to put something special on for Reggie. It wasn't well known that Reggie was allowed internal visits every three months. They enjoyed these times just sitting, eating and chatting about all the business and old times, whilst sipping Kaliber non-alcoholic lager. If there was any of the food left over, the twins would insist that it went to the other patients, just to give them a little bit extra.

I never knew when Reggie was going to visit Ron, it was all kept very hush-hush because of the security aspect. Reggie was always handcuffed inside the prison van. It didn't matter if, at the time, he was being held in Leicester Prison or Parkhurst on the Isle of Wight. The officers would spirit him out under cover and then spirit him back again before anyone could find out. You just never knew when he was going to visit Ron until the day before, or even sometimes the same day. I didn't always have time to take the food up, so I would phone the catering manager at Broadmoor to organise something and pay for it by cheque on the next visit.

They used to leave the bill at the gate house and I'd settle up when I got there. Ron loved those times he had with Reggie alone. The following day, he would eagerly tell me all about their visit.

Life and Death in Broadmoor

In all my years with Ron, I never saw the twins together. I would have loved to have seen them sitting in the visiting hall together eating lobster, sipping beer and arguing. Internal visits with Reggie were one of the few pleasures that Ronnie had left, and God knows he didn't have many. In one of Ronnie's more lethargic moods, he once told me that he thought it would have been kinder to hang him. He felt being locked away for so many years was like a slow torture. What a strange twist of fate. Long ago, when Ron was a boy, he asked his Aunt Rose why his eyebrows met in the middle. She replied, 'That means you are born to hang, Ronnie, love.'

I played my part by trying to keep Ron in the style to which he had become accustomed in other ways, too. In the end, I found myself under arrest by the Thames Valley Police, accused of bribery and corruption. At the time, of course, I denied everything, but I have to admit now that I did pass money to a number of nurses in exchange for favours for Ron. I always paid them with a business cheque from the luxury car-hire service that I was running at the time called 'Silver Ladies'.

Ronnie wanted me to pay the officers with cash, but I said that I preferred to pay them by cheque; that way, if anything went wrong, I had evidence to prove that they had worked for me. I had to cover my arse, some way or another.

After my arrest, the police carried out a major inquiry. Broadmoor had their own internal investigation, too, resulting in two staff members being forced to quit. Only now after Ron's death can I admit that I did pay some officers large sums of money for making Ron's life easier. £500 here, £1,000 there, depending on what favour Ron had asked of them. Some of them preferred gifts like portable televisions or microwave ovens rather than money, which drove me mad because I was the one who had to go and buy them. Not content with just a gift, they were always so particular about what they wanted by specifying makes, models and even catalogue numbers. Sometimes I would be shopping all day in the pouring rain, trudging from shop to shop to get it right.

Broadmoor's security is legendary — security cameras, wardens and snarling dogs. However, there was a blind spot. And guess what? Ron knew where it was!

I never used to do anything quite as dramatic as arranging secret rendezvous with 'friendly' staff at the dead of the night. It was quite simply done just before a visit. But to any passer-by it must have seemed all very cloak-and-dagger stuff, with shady-looking men loitering about in the car park talking to me out of the corner of their mouths, ready with a car boot open.

Whenever you think of furtive meetings, you always associate them with meeting under the clock at Waterloo station, with a red carnation in your buttonhole or a copy of the *Times* under your arm. We had our own Waterloo. The only blind spot surrounding Broadmoor was beneath the ghostly white statue of an angel deep in the grounds, in the shadow of its high walls. To get there, you drive up the tree-lined private road towards the main building. As you approach the main doors you bear left towards the overflow car parks at the side of Broadmoor.

Life and Death in Broadmoor

It is there that you will find the ghostly white statue where I had my secret rendezvous.

At times, the boot of my car resembled Santa's sleigh on Christmas Eve, stuffed full of portable TVs, electric organs and microwave ovens. All that was missing was a freshly plucked turkey! I never minded ferrying stuff to and fro because I knew this enabled Ron to have what he wanted in Broadmoor, including phone calls at one o'clock in the morning.

One night I was half asleep when the phone rang. In a daze, I reached for the receiver. On the end of the line was a gruff voice. 'Is that you, Kate? I've got a phone call for ya.'

I didn't recognise the voice. I couldn't work out who it was. I thought it was a crank call. 'Who's this speaking?' I snapped.

'Never mind who this is ...'

At this point he must have passed the phone over.

'Can you hear me, Kate? I've got to make it quick,' Ron whispered. 'I just had to talk to you, just for a minute.'

Ron didn't need to talk to me about anything in particular. I think he just wanted to hear a familiar voice. Someone who cared maybe. But that one phone call alone cost Ron a portable television.

I continued bribing the screws for years. Or, should I say, Ron continually bribed the screws, with me carrying out Ron's orders as the middle-man. But it all came to an abrupt end early one morning in the sleepy village of Headcorn in Kent, where I was staying with Harry, my best friend and ex-husband, in his cottage.

The Twins: Free at Last

There was a loud bang on the front door. I ran to the bedroom window and tore the curtains open, ready to shout at whoever it was making a noise at such an ungodly hour. I took a breath and held it. I saw the two plain-clothed policemen standing in the doorway. I knew they were the Old Bill straight away. Their suits, really shabby compared to Ron's, were crumpled where they had obviously been sitting in their car waiting for me.

I called out to Harry in a hushed voice, 'It's the Old Bill. I'm not here if they want me.'

I knew it could only be trouble. I just had a gut feeling about it. When Harry opened the door they introduced themselves as being from the Thames Valley Police and asked for Mrs Kate Kray. Harry said that I was not there and that he did not know where I was. They obviously did not believe him. They said they would wait.

Harry said, 'Please your fucking selves,' then slammed the door.

The Old Bill weren't bothered. They are used to playing a waiting game. They made their way back to their unmarked police car and settled in for the long wait ahead of them.

Before I spoke to the police, I thought it was better to speak to Ron. He was bound to know what was going on.

I phoned Broadmoor straight away and got a message to Ron. He told me to give them a swerve and see him immediately.

I scoffed my breakfast and got ready for the visit.

I knew the Old Bill were still waiting for me outside

the front of the house, so I decided to sneak out the back way. But there was a problem. The back gate was jammed. There was no way out. I had no choice. There was only one thing left to do — climb over the fence. A simple thing to do if you are a ten-year-old boy, which I wasn't! I reached up and grabbed the top of the rickety wooden fence. I clutched hold of it. Something felt slimy in between my fingers. I jumped back and looked at my hands. They were covered in green moss and, to top it all, I had broken a finger nail.

I got a foot-hold in the fence, swung my leg over the top and ripped my tights on a rusty spike. There I was, perched on the top of Harry's fence, my arse in the air and my tights torn to shreds. I was looking down the alley ready to jump down and, to my horror, standing at the end of the alley were the two police officers. Their hands were on their hips and a 'what-the-fuck-do-you-think-you're-doing?' look was written all over their faces.

'Mrs Kray, we need to talk to you,' they smirked.

What could I say? They had me 'bang to rights'.

I made an embarrassing and not very dignified jump from the top of the fence. My bag and its entire contents were strewn everywhere.

After the officers helped me retrieve my make-up bag from all over the muddy alley, they arrested me for bribery and corruption and took me to Berkshire Police Station. They questioned me for hours. While I was in custody, the police went back to Harry's and took away all the books and diaries in connection with my car-hire business.

The Twins: Free at Last

When the officers came into the interrogation room and produced the books, I wasn't bothered. Weeks before, I had forged entries in the diary of bogus pick-ups at Heathrow Airport. I knew that I had covered myself and the bribed staff at Broadmoor, so the Old Bill wouldn't be able to prove anything. But I was very glad I had used my head and covered my arse by paying the officers from my business account.

The newspapers had a field day saying that Ronnie and I had been arrested for bribery and corruption. It was true. I had been arrested for bribery and corruption but, when the police went to interview Ron, he told them to piss off and laughed at them, saying, 'What are you going to do — put me in prison?'

He was right — there was nothing the authorities could do to him. But they could do a lot to me. They went through all my bank accounts with a fine tooth comb but they drew a blank. This frustrated them as they desperately wanted to pin something on me because, by getting at me, they thought they would get at Ron.

It must be every copper's ambition to nail a Kray. Apart from adding Brownie points to their promotional prospects, I suppose it's something to brag about in the police canteen. They investigated just about everybody and left no stone unturned. Try as they might, they didn't succeed and, boy, did they try.

After the police dropped all the charges, Ron wanted to celebrate and asked me to bring a huge seafood banquet into Broadmoor. Ron loved seafood. He often asked me to go shopping for him. I used to get him all sorts: lobster, jellied eels, tins of crab, and his favourite — tins of sardines.

I once took twelve tins of sardines in olive oil into Broadmoor. I could not imagine what the hell he wanted with all those tins of sardines, so I asked him, 'What the fuck are you doing with all those sardines?'

Ron howled with laughter. 'I'm eating them. What the fuck do you think I'm doing with them? Smothering my body in the olive oil and trying to slip through the bars?'

This was not a rare moment of fun and laughter that we shared together in Broadmoor, but probably one that Ron would repeat to many a visitor as he thought it was just so funny.

Apart from seafood, Ron also liked good clothes. It was important for him to look good because it kept his self-respect and self-esteem which he always valued. Ron loved shoes. He thought nothing of spending £400 on crocodile shoes. I used to shop in Bond Street for them in a specialist shop called Fratelli Rossetti. Each time I went I had to buy two pairs — one black, one brown.

On one occasion I had spent nearly a grand on two pairs of crocodile shoes. They were the loafer style with two little tassels on the front. However, when Ron appeared on a visit wearing them, they were minus the tassels.

I said, 'Your shoes ... they look different. What have you done to them?'

'I've pulled those soppy tassels off,' he replied.

I shrieked, 'But they cost £400 a pair.'

'It doesn't matter how much they cost, Kate, I didn't like them.'

On one of my many visits to Broadmoor, I took Ron

The Twins: Free at Last

a beautiful silk tie. I had been out shopping in the West End and had a brilliant day, so I decided I would buy Ron a little present. I toured around the posh stores looking for something special when I eventually found a gorgeous silk tie. It was just the job and I knew Ronnie would love it. The very next morning, I took it up to him. When you take anything into a patient in Broadmoor you are not allowed to hand the item directly to them. It has to be put in a specially designed strong box. The box is then taken on to the ward and opened in front of the patient, then searched. This is to discourage anyone from smuggling anything inside the institution.

When I arrived on my visit, I put the silk tie into the strong box. Then I made my way over to the visiting hall where Ron was waiting for me. I had told him on the telephone the night before that I had bought him a pressie. He loved presents and would get all excited.

When I reached the visiting hall, the first thing he asked me was, 'What's my pressie?'

'A lovely silk tie,' I whispered. 'It's Giorgio Armani.'

Ron's face was blank. 'Giorgio Armani! Do I know him?'

'No,' I said, 'It's Giorgio Armani.'

Ron still didn't know what I meant. He was so oblivious of designer labels, he asked in all innocence, 'Didn't he like the tie, then?'

I screamed with laughter. So did Ron when I explained.

When Ron was ill, the staff at Broadmoor allowed me to go

Life and Death in Broadmoor

to his room in the new block occasionally. I never went to the old block, Taunton Ward, which was like an old Victorian nut house.

There was nothing modern about it. For years, Ron had the unenviable task of slopping out. It wasn't until the beginning of 1991 that Ron was moved to the new block. The name of the ward was Abingdon. It was meant to house all the high-profile prisoners, such as Ronnie, Sutcliffe and the Stockwell Strangler.

The new Abingdon ward, opened by Princess Diana in 1991, was set apart from the old asylum, a red-brick building looking just like a Medical Centre. I asked Ron if he saw Princess Diana that day. He was disappointed and said that he had been kept well away from the Princess because he was a high-profile prisoner. The building she opened was divided into two parts. In the middle was a small visiting area, sparsely furnished with two low coffee tables and two easy chairs.

As you walked into the main entrance you went straight into the visiting area. Directly in front of you was a big window with unbreakable glass. Outside, under the window, was a huge pond filled with Koi carp. This was, I suppose, meant to be therapeutic for the patients.

You are only allowed on to the ward when the patients are in the depths of their illness and only two patients are allowed in this visiting room at one time. The visitors are restricted as well. You are searched more thoroughly; all sharp objects are confiscated to avoid patients inflicting injuries to themselves or others. Money was also restricted, with only enough for a cup of coffee

The Twins: Free at Last

from the staff vending machine being allowed. The whole place is saturated with guards on full alert because they know the patients could turn violent at any time.

Ron much preferred it on Abingdon Ward. He said it was much more civilised. He even had his own toilet and wash basin in his cell. Isn't it strange what we take for granted on the outside? When we look through a window, we sometimes don't see for looking.

When Ron first moved to Abingdon Ward, the thing he talked about for weeks was how, for the first time in over 20 years, he could look through a window without the bars. He thought it was marvellous that the glass was unbreakable, so there was no need for bars.

'I'm not like a caged animal any more,' he said.

His room was furnished quite nicely, or as well as could be expected under the circumstances. It had a peach-coloured bedspread and matching curtains and carpet. Standing in the corner was a small oak wardrobe, where, hanging neatly in rows, were Ron's suits.

On a small shelf stood his TV and video recorder. In fact, he had all the things he wanted to make his life as comfortable as possible. Perhaps I'm giving the wrong impression. All these things did not come out of the taxpayer's pockets. His room didn't come fully furnished. Ron bought everything except the bed himself.

Broadmoor patients are not normally allowed to remain in their own rooms all day. It's Broadmoor policy to get the patients out of bed and doing some kind of activity or work for most of the day. Unless they have a job, they must go into an appointed area, usually the day-room, or if the patient feels angry or upset, he can go into the quiet room to cool off.

For Ron, it was slightly different. Ron had not been off the ward for 12 years. When I visited him on one occasion the doctor asked if he could see me for a moment. He had something he wanted my help with. He thought it would be a good idea to get Ron off the ward and they needed my help to do it. They had told him that they wanted him to take a job. Ron's reply was to tell them to piss off. He said, 'I'm not weaving fucking baskets for no one.'

They also suggested that he should try to do some gardening, but he refused. They thought I might have some influence on him. When I spoke to him, I said, 'Why don't you go out into the garden and get some fresh air? You will be able to have a fag and be on your own.'

Ron thought about it and, reluctantly, he agreed. 'I'll give it one day. Just one,' he said.

He started off out on the allotment hoeing between the spring vegetables. To his surprise, he enjoyed it so much that, in the end, he was working outside for three days a week. Two days on the allotment and the other day he spent watering the plants. He continued doing this for months. He looked better for it and he loved it.

After the initial novelty wore off, Ron's idea of gardening was to sit in the sun having a fag. But at least it got him outside, although he would only do it when the weather was nice.

At that time he began a friendship with two black twin sisters called Jennifer and June Gibbons. They were

The Twins: Free at Last

known as the 'Silent Twins' because, for many years, they did not talk to anyone except each other and, when they did, no one could understand a word they said. It was as if they had a secret language and they communicated telepathically. Ron really liked them, and he used to get me to send them flowers on their birthday. He was terribly upset when one of the twins, Jennifer, died.

Ron's work experience as a gardener ended as quickly as it began. He said to me one day out of the blue, 'I'm not going to work in the gardens any more, Kate.'

I was very disappointed. He seemed so settled. 'Why not?' I asked.

He looked at me with a dead-pan expression and, in an indignant voice, he said, ''Cos paper boys get paid more than me. I only get £12 a week.'

I couldn't argue with that, could I?

Back on the ward, some of the other patients used to get on his nerves by asking him for cigarettes and hanging around him constantly wanting to be his friend. When he wasn't feeling too good, it drove him nuts. The staff recognised this and were good enough to allow Ron to go into his own room when, and if, he wanted to.

He didn't pay for this privilege. The staff knew when Ron needed time to be alone without being pestered. They said it was for Ron's benefit, but I really do think it was for their own. Perhaps a pacified lion is better than an angry one.

A lot has been said about Ron and his sex life. When I was first with Ron we discussed his homosexuality, but he always insisted that he was bisexual. I did not have any reason to disbelieve him. It didn't matter a damn to me. I liked him as a person. Many women loved Ron and he loved women. He didn't fancy them. He loved their company. Before he was sentenced, he nearly married a girl called Monica. She was his girlfriend for three years and he told me he really loved her.

In the past, he did used to have sex with girls but said he preferred young men. Looking at a masculine man like Ron I found it hard to understand, but he just winked and said, 'You can't say you don't like oranges until you've tried one.'

He did like his little sayings and, more often than not, I had an answer for them. 'Well, I don't like fruit very much, and I certainly don't like fucking oranges.'

So, in a round about sort of way, it was my way of telling him that I was straight. He never asked me but I assumed he already knew. But, like most men, he found it difficult to talk about 'womanly' things. He enjoyed the softness of a woman, and the gentleness only women have.

One of the things Ron hated most was camp men. He despised them and would not tolerate any nonsense around him. He may have been homosexual, but Ron was a very masculine man.

I know he used to have sexual relationships in Broadmoor because he told me he did — often. I knew when he was interested in someone because he would tell me to buy a Gucci man's watch. He would wink at me with a sparkle in his eye and whisper, 'A Gucci watch always works.'

The Twins: Free at Last

He told me that many great men, such as leaders and statesmen, had been homosexuals. He quoted people like Lawrence of Arabia and Oscar Wilde.

Then, one day, right out of the blue he said to me, 'Kate, you have got one chance to ask me any question you like about my sexuality and I will give you a straight answer.'

Knowing he was serious that I would only get one shot to ask him really personal questions, I had to be careful not to go in too strong. So, initially, I asked skirting questions like what sort of men he liked. He said he preferred men in their early 20s, slim and good looking. Then I asked him the big question, one that had been bothering me and, I'm sure, everyone else.

I wasn't sure how to put it. I did not want to ask the question in a vulgar or crude way, but how do you ask someone in a polite way if they are the dominant partner in a relationship or if they are they are the passive one? There was only one thing for it, so I just blurted it out.

'Are you the giver or the taker?'

For a moment, Ron said nothing. Then a broad smile spread across his face.

'The giver, Kate, only the giver,' he whispered.

Up until that moment, I always found it difficult to imagine Ron with another man but, when he said he was the 'giver', a million pictures flashed through my mind. I threw my hands up and my facial expression said it all. There are just some things that don't require an answer.

I suppose the reason why he had said I could ask him anything I wanted on that occasion was because he had a little piece of crumpled paper in his pocket. He rummaged about in his pocket and handed it to me. Carefully, I unfolded it. It was the result of an Aids test. 'Negative'. I looked at him and he smiled.

'I knew you would never ask me to have a test, so I thought I would surprise you.'

I could see that he was in a good mood and was open to more questions. I was on a roll, so I decided to make the most of it. I thought I would chance my arm and ask him if he had ever snogged any of the blokes he went with. He looked at me and scowled. I couldn't imagine Ronnie kissing another man but I felt compelled to ask. He looked at me in complete disgust and snapped, 'Leave it out, Kate. I have never kissed a man.'

I suppose the Gucci watches Ron bought to seduce his conquests inevitably worked because the watches always disappeared. I never got any of them back. I imagine half of the patients in Broadmoor walking about wearing Gucci watches, or at least the young men among them.

On one of our visits he told me he had his eye on this black boy called Mohammed. He was on the same ward as Ron. Mohammed was a tall, good-looking lad in his early 20s. Ron was smitten with him. Every day he would go to the shower block to watch Mohammed take a shower. This went on for months and months. When I used to go on a visit, after we got business out of the way we talked about everyday things. The subject eventually got round to Mohammed in the shower.

Ron never used to take a shower at the same time as

him, but he would just happen to be in the shower block. He took great delight in watching the water run down Mohammed's black skin. His eyes shone when he talked about him.

'All those little droplets of water running down his black body looks so beautiful,' Ron said.

Then, one day, he whispered to me, 'Get me a Gucci, Kate.'

I knew then that Ron had made progress with Mohammed. Black, brown or even yellow, Ron didn't care about the colour of anyone's skin. He wasn't prejudiced and would not tolerate anyone around him who was. Some of the people Ron met, he liked. Some he despised. One man Ron despised was Ron Saxon. My Ron had three black friends in the hospital. Mohammed was one of them, the other two being Cleveland Jones and Paul Wilson.

They were not only Ron's friends but also Saxon's. Saxon would use them to fetch and carry for him, especially after he suffered a heart-attack. They really liked him and Ron obviously thought that Saxon appreciated what they did for him.

But one day, when Ron commented to Saxon about how good they'd been to him, Saxon merely said, 'They're black bastards. They're OK, but only good enough to be used.'

Ron was horrified. Racial prejudice was one of the things he hated most in the world. He told me that if Saxon had been a younger man, he would have hurt him. After that, Ron — my Ron — would have nothing to do with him. Saxon had a second heart-attack and died, and Ron

Life and Death in Broadmoor

refused to go to the funeral at Broadmoor. The only people who went were the three black boys.

'It just goes to show,' said Ron. 'It just proves to me how ignorant people can be, however old they are. They get old and they are still ignorant. I hate fascists. If Ron Saxon can see from beyond the grave — and I think he can — he would have seen those three coloured boys coming back to the ward after paying their respects to him at his funeral. And he would have seen tears in their eyes.'

It upset Ron a lot and it prompted him to write this poem:

> We are all born the same
> From God we all came
> Coloured, White or Jew
> We are all God's children, not just a few
> We should all be brothers
> And think of others
> Then, to God, we will all be true.

Coming from a half-caste family myself, I also hate racial discrimination. Looking back on it now, I think that Ron and I had a lot in common. That is probably why we got on so well. Not only were our views on lots of subjects the same, but I made him laugh when everyone else around him was always so serious.

When I first met Ron, he never used to smile much. He always took things so seriously. I remember the first time I actually saw him cry — with laughter.

We were talking about whether or not men or

women could bear the most pain. Ron insisted that men were the stronger sex. I disagreed. I looked down at his strong fist. Right across the top was a deep red scar. I asked him how he got it. He looked at me out of the corner of his eye and smirked. 'To prove a point,' he whispered.

He explained that one night he put a red-hot poker on a man's face, prompting someone to remark that Ron could give pain but not take it. He was furious when he heard that. Later that night at the pub, Ron was determined to make a point. He put his hand on the bar, pulled out a big knife and stabbed the razor-sharp blade deep into the back of his hand. Without flinching, he proceeded to tear it open, severing the veins. Blood splattered everywhere.

'Yuk! That's disgusting,' I said. 'But women can stand more pain than that, especially this woman. Look, I'll show ya.' I held my hand out in front of him.

Ron looked puzzled. He had been inside for so long he knew nothing about false finger nails. I took hold of the nails one by one and proceeded to rip them out of my finger tips. Ron winced and covered his eyes as each nail fell into the ashtray.

'Stop it, stop it,' he cringed.

I laughed. 'Do you give in? Can women stand more pain than men?'

'They are not real finger nails. What the fuck are they?' Ron asked.

I handed him an inch-long painted nail.

'Well, I never,' he sighed. 'What's happening in the world? False finger nails, eh? You little fucker, Kate,' he laughed.

Life and Death in Broadmoor

That's one thing Ron never lacked — humour. We laughed together a lot. When the BSE beef scare was in all the newspapers, he could not wait for me to go on a visit. As I walked towards him in the visiting hall, he said, 'Kate, Kate, I am never going to eat beef again. You know why? Because it drives you mad!'

I looked at him. I could not believe what he had just said. 'But, Ron, you're already mad … you're in Broadmoor.'

He scowled for a minute. I thought he was going to go into one. Then his eyes softened and a broad smile lit up his face,

'Oh yeah,' he laughed.

REG'S DREAM

*M*y dream is to be recognized first as a man and eventually as author, poet and philosopher. I could never truly regret the path I have trodden. If I did I would betray my brother, my friends and myself.

Top: An early still from the film *The Magic Box*, in which Ron Kray acted. Ron is shown here second from right – you can already recognise the profile that was to become so famous.

Below left: Ron was always an animal lover.

Below right: Reg and Charlie in the early days.

Top: Ron is pictured here with Barbara Windsor and other close friends.

Below: The famous picture of Ron and Reg being driven away to prison after being found guilty at the Old Bailey.

ROYAL ALBERT HALL

C. S. TAYLOR

Manager

JACK CAPPELL

PRESENTS AN INTERNATIONAL
BOXING TOURNAMENT

TUESDAY, DECEMBER 11th 1951

Doors open 6.45. ·Commence 7.30. ·Matchmaker: JOHN S. SHARPE

10 (3-min.) Rounds International Lightweight Contest at 9.11

TOMMY McGOVERN

Lightweight Champion of Great Britain. Versus

ALLAN TANNER

(British Guiana). Sensationally defeated Ellis Ask, Tony Lombard

---

8 3-min. Rds. Welterweight at 10.10

JACKIE | CHRISTIAN
BRADDOCK v **CHRISTENSEN**
(Manchester) | (Denmark)

8 3-min. Rds. Bantamweight at 8.9

RON | JIMMY
JOHNSON v **CARDEW**
(Bethnal Green) | (Holloway)

8 3-min. Rds. Middleweight at 11.9

JIMMY | JIMMY
DAVIS v **JAMES**
(Bethnal Green) | (Trinidad)

6 3-min. Rds. Welterweight at 10.9

LEW | CHARLIE
LAZAR v **KRAY**
(Aldgate) | (Bethnal Green)

---

8 3-min. Rds. International Cruiserweight Contest at 12.10

JOHNNY McGOWAN v ERIC JENSEN

Central Area Champion   Light-heavyweight Champion of Denmark

---

6 3-min. Rds Lightweight Contest

REG | BOB
KRAY v **MANITO**
(Bethnal Green) | (Clapham)

6 3-min. Rds. Lightweight Contest.

RON | BILL
KRAY v **SLINEY**
(Bethnal Green) | (Kings Cross)

Special Ringside 63/-

PRICES: 42/- 30/- 21/- 15/- 10/6 5/- 2/6

Betting Strictly Prohibited

Rights of admission reserved

Tickets from: PHIL COREN (Box Office Manager) GER 1742
Jack Cappell Promotions (GER 1742-3-4) Royal Albert Hall (Ken 8212).

A rare boxing poster, showing all three Kray brothers on the same bill.

Ron and Lord Boothby. Ron told me that Boothby was a kinky lord with lots of boyfriends.

Top: A young Ron on a visit to some stables.

Below: Business cards of the twins and of Charlie Kray.

J. LEVINSKY & ASSOCIATES

Charles Kray
CONSULTANT

REGISTERED BAILIFFS TO THE COUNTY COURTS; DEBT INVESTIGATION FOR DTI.
CUSTOMS AND EXCISE; DEBT ADJUSTING/COUNSELLING; DEBT COLLECTING;
CREDIT REFERENCE AGENCY; CONSUMER CREDIT

479 ROMAN ROAD, BOW, LONDON E3 5LX   TEL: 081 980 6829   FAX: 081 983 3802

KRAYLEIGH ENTERPRISES

DEBT INVESTIGATION SERVICES

JACK LEIGH   ☎ 01-981 6312

Top: Pictured here are the Clarke brothers: Ron made them literally bop till they dropped the night before the twins were arrested…

Below: Even years after their heyday, the twins' reputation was as strong as ever. This is a postcard that was recently distributed around London bars.

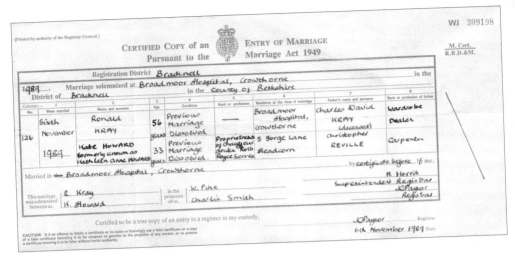

WJ 309198

CERTIFIED COPY of an **ENTRY OF MARRIAGE**
Pursuant to the Marriage Act 1949

M. Cert.
R.B.D.&M.

Registration District *Bracknell* in the

1989. Marriage solemnized at *Broadmoor Hospital, Crowthorne*
District of *Bracknell* in the *County of Berkshire*

No.	When married	Name and surname	Age	Condition	Rank or profession	Residence at the time of marriage	Father's name and surname	Rank or profession of father
126	Sixth November 1989	Ronald KRAY	56 years	Previous Marriage Dissolved	—	Broadmoor Hospital, Crowthorne	Charles David KRAY (deceased)	Wardrobe Dealer
		Kate HOWARD formerly known as Kathleen Anne HOWARD	33 years	Previous Marriage Dissolved	Proprietress of Chauffeur driven Rolls Royce Service	5 Forge Lane Headcorn	Christopher REVILLE	Carpenter

by certificate before me,
M. Harris
Superintendent Registrar

Married in the *Broadmoor Hospital, Crowthorne*

This marriage was solemnized between us, { R. Kray / K. Howard } in the presence of us, { W. Pine / Charlie Smith }

JPaynor
Registrar

Certified to be a true copy of an entry in a register in my custody,

JPaynor   Registrar
6th November 1989   Date

My wedding photos and certificate.

LORD BOOTHBY:
THE TRUTH

*'Boothby was a kinky lord
with lots of pretty boyfriends.
But he was involved in things more sinister.'*

Ronnie Kray

I n the 1960s, Lord Boothby MP took the *Mirror* newspaper to court over his alleged affair with Ron. At the time, there was a national outcry. Afraid of saying goodbye to his political career, Boothby strenuously denied the allegations. Palms were greased in the highest circles, money changed hands at an alarming rate, and the result was that Boothby was awarded £40,000 for libel.

Obviously, I would have been far too young to remember anything about the Press stories, but the majority of the time Ron liked to talk about the old days — after all,

The Twins: Free at Last

they were all he had left. The life he had in Broadmoor was just an existence, although he always tried to make the best of it; nothing really happened, every day was the same. He was eager to tell me about his life on the outside when he had been free. Of course, there were times when he didn't want to talk, and then he'd snap at me that it was 'all in the past'. But, for some reason, one day on a visit, Ron was adamant that he wanted to tell me all about a man called Leslie Holt.

Normally, when Ron talked about the past it was usually because something had jogged his memory — and what a memory he had. It was sharp as a razor, despite his illness. As he talked, it was as if in his mind he'd gone back to those days. He could remember every detail.

This particular day, something had come up in the newspaper about Lord Boothby, so Boothby was on Ron's mind when I visited him.

As soon as he walked into the visiting hall, I sensed he was in a foul mood. It was the look on his face. Someone was in for it — hopefully not me. When Ron was gunning for someone he called them 'slags and rats' and on this visit there were quite a few 'slags and rats' being thrown about.

For a change, it was not me who had upset him. All of Ron's real friends have, at one time or another, been a 'slag and a rat'. Me included. Indeed, you weren't anyone to Ronnie Kray unless he had called you that. This particular day it was Boothby's turn, and it didn't matter that he had been a Lord. To Ron, he was still a 'slag and a rat'.

Ron didn't differentiate between a dustman and a

Lord Boothby: The Truth

Lord. To him, they were all the same — potential earners.

I gave Ron his fags and fumbled in my bag for a light. As I struck the match to light his cigarette, out of the corner of his mouth he exhaled, sighed, lent back in his chair and continued on about Boothby.

He laughed and said that Boothby was a kinky Lord and had had lots of boyfriends, the younger the better. Ron stood up. I thought he was going to the toilet but instead he produced from his pocket a black-and-white photograph. He pointed at a fat old man sitting on a settee in what looked like a palatial apartment. Simply from the photograph, you could tell the man had class. It wasn't just his Saville Row suit that gave it away. Anyone can buy good clothes. What you cannot buy is breeding. And that's exactly what Boothby had — breeding.

'That's Lord Boothby,' Ron said, pointing at the faded print. 'And that's Leslie Holt.'

Obviously, I had heard of Lord Boothby but Leslie Holt's name didn't ring any bells with me — then again, why should it? Ron started going on and on about Holt, insisting that he was a 'no good bastard' and that he deserved to die. He was really slagging him off. I found it hard to follow what he was saying but one thing was sure — Ron hated him. At the end of the day, I didn't really have an opinion. I had never heard of Leslie Holt and told Ron I couldn't care less about him. But Ron didn't listen to a word I said. He was relentless, and was determined to tell me all about him. He explained that Holt was a vain 'nancy boy' and that he was obsessed by the disfiguring warts on his hands and feet.

The Twins: Free at Last

He was good looking, though. Good-looking enough to become one of Ronnie's boys. BINGO! For the first time, Ron had my full attention. My ears always pricked up when Ron started talking on a more personal level. I looked at Ron as he sipped his chilled lager and gently wiped his mouth. I winced. 'One of your boys? YUK!'

Ron laughed. 'Yeah, he was one of my boys — warts and all.'

Ron continued to say that Holt was also Lord Boothby's boyfriend. But that wasn't all. Holt wasn't satisfied with a gangster and a Lord. He involved one other person, creating a triangle with him in the middle. This other person was someone whom he thought would be useful to him, an eminent Harley Street doctor by the name of Gordon Kells, the man later charged with Leslie Holt's murder.

It seemed that the young Mr Holt had been swapped around like pass-the-parcel at a children's birthday party. But it was no ordinary, run-of-the-mill party. Holt had champagne ideas with a brown ale pay-packet. Big ideas that needed lovers with big bank balances. He targeted high-society pals, then blackmailed them.

But Holt had a problem — warts. Being a vain man, he hated the unsightly lumps and bumps on his hands and feet and wanted them removed, whatever the cost. But he was skint and could not afford the high costs of such an operation. He was a determined man on a mission — he had to get rid of those awful warts.

It was around this time that Holt started having the

affair with Dr Kells, the Harley Street doctor. Unable to afford Dr Kells' fees, Holt paid with his sexual favours. Dr Kells was due to remove the unsightly warts under a local anaesthetic, a simple operation for such an eminent surgeon, one that he had performed probably a thousand times before. But, mysteriously, Holt died.

Ron gave one of his knowing smirks. I was taken aback.

'People don't die from something like that,' I gasped.

Ron shrugged his shoulders.

I did not understand immediately what Ron was trying to tell me. His eyes narrowed. He held my arm, pulled me close and whispered, 'You silly girl, you don't really think he died from a local anaesthetic do you? The doctor was the Patsy.'

I knew what the term 'Patsy' meant — a mug who takes the blame for something — but I didn't understand what Ron meant by saying that the doctor was the 'Patsy'.

'What do you mean "he was the Patsy"?' I asked.

Ron realised he had already said more than he should. 'Oh nothing,' he snapped. 'Forget all about it.'

He had done it again. Only telling me part of the story. I became very irritable. 'Tell me more,' I insisted.

But Ron clammed up and was having none of it. I tried my best to get him to tell me more, but he wouldn't. In the seven years I was with Ron, he never brought the subject up again. But the words 'the doctor was the Patsy' has always stuck in my mind.

Ron obviously didn't want the story coming out

whilst he was alive, but he gave me that information in Broadmoor that day for a reason. I had a gut feeling that he was trying to tell me something. I acquired all the newspaper cuttings on Leslie Holt, and was shocked by what I discovered. Leslie Holt had died mysteriously, very mysteriously, from a massive overdose of Methohexitone. It was Doctor Kells, the Harley Street surgeon, who had administered the fatal injection.

That was it. That was what Ron was trying to tell me. The doctor was the 'Patsy'. I was intrigued.

After I had finished reading all the cuttings, I smiled to myself. In his own way, Ron had led me on to something that had long been forgotten. The old fox. He knew I would remember what he had said. He also knew that I would find out more. He once said that nobody could get anything over on me, that I was as sharp as a tack. Well, he was right. I don't profess to know the whole story about Leslie Holt. I will let you decide for yourselves what really happened to the vain nancy boy covered in warts.

Ron's association with Lord Boothby has been well documented, as has the libel case Boothby took out against the *Mirror* after it exposed their love affair. Boothby always denied the affair. In those days, homosexuality was illegal for one thing, but it would have also destroyed his political career. Ron always admitted that he was bisexual; he didn't give a damn that it was against the law — since when did breaking the law ever bother Ronnie Kray? More importantly, he loved the idea of having a relationship with a famous peer who was once Winston Churchill's Parliamentary Secretary.

Lord Boothby: The Truth

While Boothby was suing the newspaper, Ron had to deny the affair. In close circles, however, he readily admitted to it as he thought it was a coup to get a Minister under his belt and, even better still, a Minister who was a Lord.

Years later Boothby found himself in court again, denying an affair with Holt, but when Holt started to blackmail Boothby it was Ron to whom Boothby turned for help. But Leslie Holt was greedy; he was already trying to blackmail the surgeon and Boothby, but made a fatal mistake of chancing his arm, and his life, by trying to blackmail Ron over his affair with Boothby in the 1960s.

Ron was sharp and knew that his friendship with Boothby would come in handy for something. Little did he realise that his association with Boothby created waves in high places and later led to repercussions, which was the reason why both he and Reggie were made an example of with 30-year recommended prison sentences.

As I've already said, lots of questions have been asked why the twins received such a long sentence for one murder each. The reason was political. Reg and Ron climbed the social ladder and mingled with royalty, MPs and Lords and Ladies, soon finding themselves way out of their depth. After the murders of Jack the Hat and George Cornell, their high-society friends became scared. Suddenly, it was no longer trendy to mingle with dangerous gangsters. They began to give the twins a wide berth.

Whispers reverberated throughout Parliament. It was only a matter of time before faceless men in authority felt it was their duty to make an example of them by giving them each a life sentence. The Judge recommended that they should each serve 30 years before they were considered for parole. At their trial in March 1969, at the Old Bailey, Mr Justice Melford Stevenson said to Ron, 'I am not going to waste words on you. The sentence is that of life imprisonment. In my view, society has earned a rest from your activities.'

For Mr Justice Melford Stevenson — known as 'The Hanging Judge' — it was the moment he had been waiting for, the climax of the longest murder trial in the history of Britain's Central Criminal Court, a high spot in his long legal career. The Krays had stood in the dock facing their accusers for 39 days. It took the jury just six hours and fifty-four minutes to decide their guilt and, in sentencing them to life, with a recommendation of 30 years apiece, Judge Melford Stevenson was handing out the longest sentence for murder ever known at the Old Bailey.

The government at the time hoped it would put the fear of God into any other gangster who got too big for his boots. 'It doesn't matter who you are or how big you get, we will always win' — that was the message.

Judges do not come from the East End, and they don't go to comprehensive schools. Judges and MPs often come from public schools. The twins had the ability to attract people from all walks of life. Having power and money is one thing; Reg and Ron had plenty of that. High society has power and money, as well as the all-important breeding. If you haven't got the breeding, money and power can't buy it. You can only skirt around the edges of high society. Once you try to infiltrate it, they close ranks.

Lord Boothby: The Truth

Although they loved flirting with the danger that surrounded the twins, when Reg and Ron dared to cross their line they were slapped down and made an example of. And, boy, did they make an example of them.

The newspaper headlines read: BOOTHBY AND THE GANGSTER!

Ron said that he roared with laughter when he read the paper. I asked him how the papers found out. He winked. 'Because we told them. That way, we had Boothby where we wanted him. I had to deny the affair to the world so Boothby felt he owed me a favour — and, boy, did we milk him.'

Leslie Holt died in September 1979 at the age of 42, after surgery to remove a wart from his big toe. Doctor Gordon Kells was charged with manslaughter. Holt was in his early 20s when he met Lord Boothby. He was a successful and glamorous young criminal who drove an Aston Martin, which Boothby bought for him, bearing his personalised number plates.

Although Lord Boothby always maintained that his relationship with Leslie Holt was not a sexual one, Ron insisted that it was, very much, a sexual relationship. And if anyone should have known, Ron did, because he was having a relationship with both of them.

Holt was one of six sons of a Shoreditch dustman. Lord Boothby was educated at Eton and Oxford. They made a highly unlikely couple — especially in those days — but Boothby and Holt formed a friendship that bridged the social gulf. It was so close that Holt's family and friends say that the Peer wanted to adopt the young cockney lad who was 37 years his junior. Boothby denied the gay affair, maintaining that they were just good friends, and he was quoted in the newspapers at the time, saying, 'It was a perfectly normal relationship. I met Leslie Holt at a boxing match. I took to him right away. He used to drop in a couple of times a year just for a chat. We were just good friends, and I enjoyed his company.'

Boothby went on to reveal at his posh home in Eaton Square, in London's Belgravia, 'I had no idea that Holt was a notorious crook and had been to jail several times.'

But Holt boasted to friends that it was Lord Boothby who had bought him his Aston Martin sports car. It was as plain as the nose on your face that Lord Boothby and Leslie Holt were gay lovers. Ron told me they were, and he should have known — he'd had affairs with both of them. Why else would Lord Boothby buy a cockney boy the most expensive car of its time. Even today, few people can afford such a luxury car — only the likes of Prince Charles and overpaid pop stars have that privilege.

Boothby was adamant and continued to deny the affair, even though Leslie Holt's mum and dad, George and Mary Holt, were taken to Lord Boothby's Eton Square house by Holt in his Aston Martin, the one that the Lord had bought for him. Holt always said that Lord Boothby was a gentleman, and was only being friendly when his parents went to his house. They sat in his beautiful apartment and drank scotch and talked for hours, but it is interesting why a man of Boothby's calibre would want to meet the local dustman. It's laughable.

Lord Boothby: The Truth

Boothby also took Holt abroad and, at one time, he was Boothby's chauffeur and they travelled overseas together. He encouraged Holt's interest in the arts; he would take him to art galleries which Holt enjoyed enormously. He always said that Boothby educated him in the finer things of life. He made friends with some of London's top barristers and had a love affair with a male executive from London's top fashion magazine.

He used to go to all the best parties and was a familiar face at London's most exclusive nightclubs.

Ron told me that Holt made no secret of being in and out of bed with many different people, and Holt told Ron that he had to put the squeeze on them to get some cash. Ron said that he had helped Holt to fence diamonds and jewels that he had stolen after having sex with his high-society friends, and that Holt was threatened on many occasions — one lover he was blackmailing threatened to have Holt's arms chopped off. But all the time Holt was one of Ron's boys, he knew that he was safe and Ron would protect him. When he was talking to Ron, Holt just laughed and said, 'What can they do about it? Nothing.'

He had become very cocky. He had blackmailed many powerful people and upset a lot more. Another one of Holt's lovers was Dr Gordon Kells, the Harley Street surgeon, who earned himself the nickname of the 'spare parts doctor' when he began a scheme to buy kidneys and other human organs from poor overseas countries for transplant surgery in Britain. His plan was heavily criticised by other doctors, but Kells ignored his colleagues. He wrote a medical paper in which he said that the more affluent

The Twins: Free at Last

society should offer to purchase, for example, a kidney from a fit man from the Third World. If the man was offered £2,000, the doctor suggested, he would be happy because, for the cost of a kidney, he would become relatively rich in his own country.

Ron said that Leslie Holt and the surgeon became lovers shortly before Holt's untimely death. Holt decided to use the surgeon as planned, to remove his unsightly warts free of charge because, if he refused, Holt threatened to expose their relationship. Dr Kells felt unable to refuse him and the operation was booked for September 1979.

Holt arrived at Dr Kells surgery at 9.00pm on a drizzly September night. The doctor tried to turn him away.

He used every excuse possible, feebly explaining that he did not feel too well himself and that, that very day, he had been knocked down by a car and had fallen off his bike and hit his head. Holt however, insisted that the surgery was done. He was due to have three warts removed from his feet and a cyst removed from behind his ear. Doctor Kells reluctantly agreed and gave him a local anaesthetic, but Holt complained about the pain, and was given an injection of what the doctor said was Valium.

Holt collapsed and was taken to hospital where he later died. The Police Scientific Officer, John Taylor, said that the tests revealed a massive overdose of Methohexitone, apparently 10 to 20 times higher than recommended. Pathologist Dr Ian West said that the use of the drug was totally inappropriate unless a doctor had an assistant to watch the patient's heart and breathing rate.

Strangely enough, two weeks before Holt's death,

Kells' mews home was broken into and valuable antiques were stolen. At his trial, the doctor said he did not want to treat the warts as he was feeling unwell. Mr Holt, who was returning to his home in Balenyffos, Dyfed in South Wales the following day, persuaded him to go ahead. He became very abusive and started shouting that he could not hang about. He wanted the operation done and he wanted it done now. He was determined to have his warts removed. The doctor reluctantly agreed for the sake of some peace and quiet.

Holt was 42 when he died.

In 1981, Dr Kells was eventually cleared by an Old Bailey jury of unlawful killing. Holt's story is a very strange tale. Ron obviously knew more than he was prepared to divulge. Maybe there was a cover up. Maybe Boothby was involved. Now that Ron, Reg, Boothby and Holt are all dead, we will probably never know...

RON ON VIOLENCE

You will get more from someone if you ask nicely. There is no need to shout – just say please and thank you. That's what I always do!

SECRETS, SCANDALS AND SKULDUGGERY

Ronnie sent literally hundreds of letters to me during our relationship, touching on dozens of different topics in his spidery, sprawling handwriting. Most of the letters were mundane — like 'Bring me two tins of sardines and a new vest.' But on the odd occasion, Ron would write a letter that revealed the truth about a secret, like the death of Freddie Mills.

Freddie Mills was one of the most idolised fighters of his day. He was found dead in suspicious circumstances slumped in his car near his Soho nightclub. He had a bullet through his eye and a fairground rifle was lying close by. A Coroner's Court returned a verdict that Mills had killed himself, but no motive for such an act ever emerged and the mystery remains unsolved until now.

The Twins: Free at Last

Freddie Mills was a pal of Ronnie's and he also listed dozens of showbusiness celebrities among his friends and was particularly close to gay 1960s singer Michael Holiday, who himself had committed suicide that same year. Ronnie and I talked about Freddie Mills during my visits to Broadmoor. Freddie was a man Ronnie really admired, a real man's man and, because they were both boxers, they had shared a sort of special bond. I know of the rumours that had been flying about that Ronnie and Freddie Mills were lovers. On one of our visits I asked Ron if that story was true. Ron said that it wasn't. Friends yes, but no sex. He said that he respected the man, as a human being and as a great fighter and, anyway, he didn't like masculine types like Mills. He liked young, slim men in their early 20s.

Ron obviously knew a lot more about the whole business than he was prepared to say openly.

Freddie Mills was killed on Saturday, 24 July 1965. He'd had a normal sort of day, quietly pottering about in his garden at his luxury home in Denmark Hill, South London, which he shared with his wife Chrissie and two daughters, Susan and Mandy. Later that evening, as usual, he went to his club, the Freddie Mills Nite Spot in Goslett Yard, Soho.

Freddie was a good host. He was the Peter Stringfellow of his day. Punters went to the club not only to see a World Champion Boxer, but to fraternise with the rich and famous. That night, Freddie was on good form and gave no indication of suicidal tendencies, as friends who were there at the time said later. On the contrary, that night champagne corks popped freely as he enjoyed what was to be his last evening alive. Nobody saw him leave the club in the early hours of that Sunday morning. He never returned home. Chrissie, his wife, was frantic with worry and went to look for him. She wished she hadn't.

She found him slumped in his car in Goslett Yard, dead. He had been shot through the eye. Ron said that half of Freddie's brain was splattered on the back seat of his car.

It was a strange case. The coroner's verdict was that he had taken his own life, but the people who knew him best said that that didn't make any sense.

All kinds of stories started circulating — stories about Freddie's alleged homosexual affairs, his supposed money troubles. People said he'd been murdered. Of course, since Ron and Reg were London's leading gangsters at the time, some people also pointed the finger at them. And the finger has remained pointed in their direction for nearly 30 years.

I asked Ron, point-blank, 'Did you kill Freddie Mills?'

Ron looked me in the eye and shook his head. 'No, I didn't kill him, I'm afraid – that's just a myth. But I did kill Cornell ...'

Whenever Ron spoke about George Cornell, his face distorted with hatred. He said that Cornell was a bully and that was one of the things he hated most. Ron said that Cornell was also a big-mouth. He was loud and brash. Ron couldn't stand him.

When we were talking about him one day, Ron stubbed his fag out in the ashtray and immediately lit another one. He was getting wound up.

'Don't get wound up, Ron,' I said.

On 9 March 1966 Ron heard that Cornell was drinking in The Blind Beggar on Whitechapel Road in East London. Ronnie told Reggie that it was about time he dealt with Cornell.

'I'm going to do the bastard tonight,' he said.

Ron washed and shaved, went to his wardrobe and chose one of his many suits which were hanging in a neat row. Carefully, he put a 9mm Mauser hand-gun in the right-hand pocket of his cashmere overcoat. He looked in the mirror and nodded his head. He felt good.

'I'll pass with a push and a pull,' he muttered.

He swaggered down the stairs and motioned to his driver.

'Let's do it.'

His driver snatched the car keys from the kitchen table and drove Ron to The Blind Beggar. It was early evening; the roads were empty. His car pulled up outside the pub. Ron got out. He shrugged his shoulders, straightened his tie and coolly walked into the pub. Cornell was sitting in the near-empty bar with two of his side-kicks. He smirked, 'Well, look who's just walked in.'

Ron never said a word. He walked towards the bar, took the gun out of his pocket, aimed at Cornell's head and fired. He was dead before he hit the carpet.

Cornell's drinking buddies dived for the floor, as

did the two or three terrified customers who had been sitting nursing their pints. The barmaid screamed. The record on the jukebox jammed and started to blast out, again and again, the line of the song it had been playing: 'The sun ain't gonna shine any more, the sun ain't gonna shine any more ...'

Ron strolled out of the pub. He was on a high. He later told me that at that moment, the moment he shot Cornell in the head, he felt fucking marvellous. Ron said that Cornell glared at him as he pulled the trigger. Ron laughed. 'His brains made a good pattern on the wall. I smelt fear on him and I loved it,' he said.

When Ronnie got back to the pub where Reggie was waiting, Ron told him what he had done. Immediately, they made their way to another pub. They went round the side entrance as they did not want to be seen and banged on the door. The landlord opened it to find Ronnie and Reggie standing there, Ronnie covered in blood. Nodding at his brother, Reggie said, 'He's just killed George Cornell.'

The landlord was scared but let them in and showed Ronnie to the bathroom. Ron took his clothes off, climbed into the bath and scrubbed himself in a bid to wash away the blood and brains. Not easy. It was nasty, sticky stuff, coating him from his hair down. Hardest of all to remove were the powder marks which had scorched Ron's hand.

He changed into fresh clothes brought from their aunt's house in Vallance Road. He washed his jewellery and watch and burnt his paper money. Ron's bloodstained clothes were stuffed into a suitcase, then taken away to be burned. Another friend, Charlie Clark, the burglar known as the Cat Man, disposed of the gun, the gun that evaded the police despite extensive searches.

Ronnie waited anxiously for news of the killing, passing the time with friends having a few drinks and a cheese sandwich. He turned on the *Nine O'Clock News* to hear that there had been a fatal shooting in the East End. He took another bite of his cheese sandwich, looked at his brother and smiled.

Later that evening, Ron was back home, fast asleep. The police hammered at his door and took him into custody for questioning. He declared his innocence. The police arranged for an immediate identity parade. Eye-witnesses, who had been in The Blind Beggar, could not — or would not — pick him out of the line up. Much to Ron's delight, he was released. The police could prove nothing. No one was talking. But they knew — as everyone who knew anything about anything in the East End knew — that Ronnie Kray had killed George Cornell.

Now Ron had really lived up to his nickname of the 'Colonel', given to him by the Firm because of the precise way in which he organised 'business' and because he loved a battle; the bloodier the better.

1967 was the year of the beginning of the end for Reg and Ron. It was also the year of what has since been described as their greatest coup: the springing of a villain called Frank Mitchell, known as the 'Mad Axeman', from Dartmoor prison.

Secrets, Scandals and Skulduggery

The strange disappearance of 'Mad Axeman' Frank is one of the legendary stories of London's gangland in the 1960s. He was one of the Kray firm's toughest heavies. An enforcer so big and so vicious no one contradicted anything he said. If on a Tuesday Frank Mitchell said it was Thursday, then it was Thursday. No one dared argue with the big nasty bastard, but he loved the twins and was a key player in their criminal empire and was prepared to do almost anything Ron and Reg commanded. Inevitably, he ended up inside as a Category 'A' hard-case prisoner, a man feared by just about every screw who ever dealt with him.

But Reg and Ron needed him out for a major job they had got planned. In a brazen operation which typified the ever-increasing power of the Kray gang, the twins organised Mitchell's escape from Dartmoor, then Britain's harshest prison.

The escape was planned with military precision. Reggie even did a recce and made a trip to Dartmoor. He contacted a friend, former World Boxing Champion Ted 'Kid' Lewis, and asked him to write to the prison Governor offering to give a talk to the cons about his boxing career and show some films of his fights. Ted mentioned that he would be accompanied by three friends. Of course, Ted had no idea why his friends wanted to visit Dartmoor.

Unbeknown to the authorities, one of them was Reggie who, just for fun, also brought along two of his friends, ex-cons with long list of convictions. An enjoyable day out was had by all — especially as the

The Twins: Free at Last

Governor treated Ted and his group to a splendid meal after the show and urged them all to 'call again'. With a straight face, Reggie assured him they'd be delighted.

Shortly afterwards, Frank Mitchell was with an outside working party when he quietly slipped away from the other prisoners. At a pre-arranged point, he met two members of the Firm, who bundled him into a car. He was back in London before he had even been missed.

He was never seen again and, to this day, his disappearance remains one of the great gangland mysteries which surrounded the Krays. The twins and members of their firm were arrested and stood trial at the Old Bailey. All were acquitted.

The story Ron told me reveals a simple, but basic, motive for the removal of Frank 'Mad Axeman' Mitchell. Ron said that once Mitchell was sprung from the nick he was put up in a nice comfortable flat near his parents, over a shop in Canning Town, in south-east London, and told to keep his head down for a few weeks until all the fuss had blown over.

When Ronnie went down to Canning Town to see him after a couple of days, he asked Mitchell if everything was all right and if there was anything in particular he wanted. Mitchell looked at him and said, 'Ron, after five years inside there's only one thing I want at the moment, and that's some crumpet.'

It was natural enough, I suppose, and Ron agreed that he would find a nice-looking prostitute who would do the business with Mitchell, at Ron's expense of course. But Ron was worried that things were still too hot and

Secrets, Scandals and Skulduggery

that a prostitute might tip-off the police about Mitchell's hide-out. He said he needed to find a brass who would not grass and Ron thought there might be a problem with the girls being frightened of going with Mitchell because of his hard-man reputation.

Mitchell got more and more restless as each day went by and kept asking Ron when they were going to bring the woman. After six days, Mitchell could wait no longer. He was really steamed up and threatened to go out and look for a tart himself. Ron warned him not to step outside or it would blow the whole operation. At the same time, he was being fed on the best steaks and any other grub he wanted. Boy, did he know his way to the pantry. He ate like there was no tomorrow. He was getting fitter and stronger by the day. But the only thing Mitchell hankered after was a woman. Reg arranged for a girl to keep him quiet and brought him Lisa, a beautiful hostess to keep him company. She tamed him for a week, but then he became restless and aggressive, pulling a knife on one of his minders. Waving his knife in the air, he demanded to see his parents, who lived nearby, and also demanded to see Ronnie. But by this time, Ron had lost interest, and no longer visited Mitchell. The final straw came when Mitchell said, 'If anything happens to me, I'll hold the Krays' mother responsible.' When Ronnie heard, he was furious. It was the final nail in his coffin.

Later that same evening, he gave the word and three shifty looking men arrived at the flat where Mitchell was staying. They told Mitchell that it was getting too hot at the small flat above the shop. He was being moved to a safe house in the country. There, he could have as many tarts as he wanted.

Mitchell sat on the sofa in the lounge smoking a fag and reading one of his porno magazines. Two of the men sat at the kitchen table playing cards. Another stood by the window keeping watch making sure the coast was clear, from time to time peeking through the net curtain. Under the cover of darkness, Mitchell was led to the waiting van. The engine was running. The driver lit his roll-up for the umpteenth time. Mitchell bent his huge torso almost in half as he climbed into the grey Commer van. The three 'faces' climbed in behind him. Once inside, the van was locked.

Ron told me later that the man who killed him said, 'Mitchell was a bugger to kill. He sat in the back of the van. At first he was chatty. Then it suddenly dawned on him. He realised it was all coming on top. He knew his life was in danger but it was too late.'

His assassin took the gun from his inside pocket and pulled back the trigger. Mitchell looked him in the eye. Nobody spoke.

Bang. The first bullet thumped into his body. He slumped forward on to his knees clutching his heaving chest. Blood oozed from the gaping wound. He gasped. His executor stood astride his helpless victim.

BANG. BANG. BANG. He emptied the clip into the lifeless body.

Ron's eyes shone as he told me that story. It was obvious he was telling me the truth. He had no reason to lie. He was already serving life so if he had killed Frank Mitchell then he would have told me. I asked Ron what had happened to Mitchell's body. He just laughed ...

REG ON DEATH

*D*eath is something we would all like to know more about, but are reluctant to meet. Life after death should be exciting, but I'm in no rush to get there. But when my time comes, I'll face the challenge just like I've faced all the other challenges in my life — head on.

TRIBUTES

Charlie Bronson

Charlie has spent 26 years in prison, 22 of those in solitary confinement. He's been locked in dungeons, he's even been in a 'Hannibal' cage. He's the most violent prisoner in the British penal system. Yet there were two people who knew how to control him, by showing him respect and a bit of human kindness. Those two people were the twins, and this is his tribute to them...

The twins to me are really like family. I love them as I love my family. I first met them in Parkhurst Jail in 1975. I was only 23 years old and they helped me through a bad time. At that time of my life I was very vicious and unpredictable. I was forever blowing these screws away. Ron and Reg seemed to understand me. Ron even more so. Later Ron and me ended up in Broadmoor, and years later I was with Reg again in Gartree. Right up until Ron died that man stood by me and helped me. He used to be able to sense when I was in one of my black moods, and he would surprise me and cheer me up.

Once, Ron got Terry Downes, the ex-World Champion boxer, to come and see me. Ron would do things like that. And Reg used to get me signed photos of the stars. Yeah, they are true humans with great warmth and humanity. Men of steel, but with feelings! Look at the good they done, then weigh it up with the bad. It's the good that shines through every time.

All the crap you read on them! Well, I would never once see any evil, only good! Sure, if a geezer was in for a slap, he got it. But a well-deserved slap it would be. Ron and Reg despised bullies! They lived by a code of honour and don't fuck with women. Don't harm kids. Don't burgle nice people. Don't mug old people on our plot. Even in prison their values were the same. Don't rob out of cons' cells. Don't bully the weak. If you want a punch-up, go smash a screw. That's the twins in a nutshell.

Me, I cried my heart out when Ron died – literally! I lost not just a friend, but a father figure. I felt a lot for Ron, as I suffer with the same sort of illness he did. It's why we were close, as we could relate to each other's black moods.

Reg. Well, Reg is the strongest man on the planet. He survives it all. What a great fighter. Remember, Reg Kray spent 33 years caged up. He lost his Mum, Dad, Twin, Charlie all his family, but he kept on and on. He dug deep! He won! Fuck anybody who says different. He's an icon. And Ronnie would be proud of Reg. It's what Ron always wanted – to see Reg freed. Ron accepted his fate like the man he was, but Reg had to get freed – and did!

Forget about the gangster element. Try and see the twins in a different light, and I swear to God you'd see two gentlemen, and believe me, you'll never see the like of them again. The mould smashed when they were born. There'll never be another like them again. Pure icons.

Total admiration and respect.

Charlie

Linda Calvey

L inda Calvey is serving life for murder. The newspapers dubbed her The Black Widow. When I approached her for a tribute to the twins, she told me stuff I had never heard before.

I was nearly your sister in law, Kate. Reg and I used to phone each other once a week – one week I'd ring him, the next week he'd ring me – we were very close. He was always sending me flowers. He sent me 2 dozen beautiful white roses once, and he used to send me perfume when I was in Durham, and gym-wear, and trainers.

The Twins: Free at Last

Then one day, out of the blue, Reg surprised me by asking me to marry him. I was taken aback, and told him it was an honour, but I had to refuse him. Funnily enough, In the same week, Charlie Bronson asked me to marry him. I said no – same as I said to Reg. I thought, Bloody hell, I've been proposed to by two of the most infamous inmates in Britain. And yet I'd been turned down by Danny Reece, the third most infamous prisoner in Britain (although I did end up marrying him).

I remained friends with Reggie up until the day he died. I'll never forget the day when I was minding my own business working in the prison shop when all of a sudden it came on the radio that Ron had died. I thought, Oh my God, Reg. I walked back into the prison wing and into the office, and asked to telephone Reg. They rang Maidstone hospital and said who it was, but the officer on the other end said Reg was seeing the Governor and would get back to me. A couple of hours later, Reggie called. I was shocked at what he told me.

He'd put in an application to be allowed to visit Ronnie in hospital. Reg had been called into the office and was handed back his application. It had been refused, the screws said, because Ron wasn't ill enough. As Reg walked back to his cell, another con opened his door, and called Reg in. He had just heard the terrible news on the radio that Ron had died.

'Reg,' he said, 'have you heard the news?' Reg was puzzled – he didn't know what the con was talking about. The authorities never had the decency to inform him. When Reg heard the news he was still holding that application –

refused because Ron was supposedly not ill enough, and there he was – dead.

Jack Binns

*I*first met Reg and Ron in Dartmoor prison in the late *'60s. I was always up to a bit of skulduggery, mainly violence. On this occasion I was sent to Dartmoor for biting a man's ear off. I met the twins on the landing. They called me 'the mad Yorkshireman'.*

They were great lads. It was Ronnie who was the domineering one. Reggie took notice. Ronnie always had the final say. Ronnie Kray was a very powerful man ...

Jack Binns
Bradford, October 2000

Joey Pyle

I met big Joey Pyle on the first visit I ever had with Ron. I had known Reggie for a while, and was nervous about meeting his brother, someone I had heard so much about. My first impression of Broadmoor, too, didn't exactly help to calm my nerves. But having got through the security checks, and having broken the ice with Ron over a cup of tea and a few pleasantries, I was feeling a little more at ease. Ron was the perfect gentleman.

Then another man joined us — a big man in a big suit — and I got up to leave. 'No, don't go,' said Ron, and introduced me to his friend. Joey Pyle. The only man who consistently visited Ron every single week of his 28

The Twins: Free at Last

years inside. Joey is an imposing man, someone you would be reluctant to approach without an introduction. His hair is black, slicked back, with grey around the sides, making him very distinguished. He has twinkling blue eyes that are soft with women and cold as ice around men.

I stood up and moved around the table so that Joe could sit next to Ron. Joe wanted to talk business. I sat back in my chair and tried not to listen but Ron wanted to include me in the conversation. He asked me to sit forward, not wanting to leave me out or make me feel uneasy.

I didn't have anything to say but Ron was always a gentleman and so aware of other people's feelings. He knew I would probably feel uncomfortable and went out of his way to put me at my ease.

When the visit had finished, Ron was taken out of the hall and turned to the left. Joe and I were escorted out and went to the right. I looked over my shoulder and noticed that Ron had stopped. He was watching me and Joe being led along the corridor. Joe put his arm around my shoulder. He turned round, smiled, and winked at Ron. 'See you later, Colonel,' he said with a saucy grin.

Ron folded his arms and smiled, too. He knew exactly what Joe was doing — teasing him.

That was in 1987. From that day on, Joey became my friend as well. Joey has always been a good business man and a man of his word. Ron told me once that when Joey Pyle gave his word, it might just as well be written in stone. Ron trusted Joey with his life.

Whenever there was a party that I had to attend, it was always Joey and his close friends whom Ron trusted to escort me. It was at these parties that I met all of Ron's firm friends. And after his death, of course, Joe had nothing but good words to say about Ron:

I knew as soon as I met Ronnie Kray he was something special and we became friends almost straight away.

It was way back in the '50s when I met him. We were only in our 20s but Ron was already a man to know. His fearsome reputation preceded him, but he was also known for his sincerity and his loyalty.

Indeed, if you made a friend of Ronnie Kray, you made a friend for life. If, on the other hand, you made an enemy of him, you paid the ultimate price. I got on all right with him, we had something in common — boxing. Initially, it was this that brought us together. We were the same age and mixed in the same circles. I went on to became a professional middleweight fighter. Ron loved boxing. He was good at it, too. So was Reggie.

Ron could have gone a long way in the boxing world, but he didn't have the discipline that boxing demanded. He had other ideas. Big ideas. He wanted to get to the top. He didn't have time for early morning jogs and workouts. He was far too impatient.

During the '50s and '60s we were always bumping into each other. I often had a drink with him in the Astor Club just off Berkeley Square. He had been off doing his bit of business and I had been doing mine.

The Astor Club was the place to go when all the

pubs were closed, therefore it was usually in the early hours of the morning that we started doing the odd bit of business together, which meant I would regularly have a drink with Reg and Ron in the East End, which was their manor. In return, they would come over to the West End to return the compliment.

Ron and I shared the same passion — good suits and monogrammed shirts. The night my son was born, Joey Junior, we had a huge party in the Astor Club. It was a night to remember.

The day Joey was sentenced to six years for drug smuggling, Ron said that he felt that that was the last time he would ever see Joey. I tried to reassure him. But he was adamant. I don't know how he knew he just did. Ron was psychic like that.

After Joey was sentenced, obviously he was no longer able to visit Ronnie, but his incarceration didn't stop him from writing. I know for a fact that they wrote to each other every week.

When Ron died, Joey was devastated. Because Joey was Category 'A' he wasn't allowed to attend Ron's funeral. I knew how Joey would be feeling. He was Ronnie's closest friend and wanted to show his respects and couldn't. It was obvious he would feel left out. Because I knew what Ronnie meant to Joey, I wanted to include him in some way. I noticed on the service sheet that Joey's name had been included in the names of people who were not able to attend. I thought Joey might like a copy of the service sheet, but they were as rare as rocking-horse shit.

On the day of the funeral sightseers were offering hundreds of pounds for a copy, especially one with the Kray name printed on it.

So, after the funeral, I photocopied my service sheet and I sent it to Joey. A few days later, a letter arrived from Joey thanking me. Attached to the letter was a poem. In the letter Joey explained that whilst he had been locked up in his cell, he felt Ron's presence and felt compelled to write the poem.

I do believe Joey, when he said that Ron came to him that night in his cell. Maybe Ron had something on his mind. Maybe he just wanted to say goodbye. Joey has never written a poem before or since; Ron, on the other hand, has had poems published.

The words in the poem are quite poignant. Joey says they're Ron's words, not his. I think it is beautiful.

The time has come to say my farewell
But there's a few things I'd like to tell
For 26 years they've kept me confined
They said I was mad and out of my mind
I never let my pals down, and I went with the grain
If that's being mad, then I must be insane
I've done some bad things and I've done some good
But I always did good before bad, if I could
I was deprived of my freedom for so many years
But feel no pity, and don't shed tears
As I'm free from the screws and that stinking cell
Free from the slop-outs, and that Broadmoor hell

The Twins: Free at Last

So feel no sadness, and please don't mourn
For I haven't left you, I'm just reborn
So Kate remember, I'm a whisper away
And we'll get it together again some day ...

Every time I read this I get goose-bumps. I really do believe that it was a message from Ron and so did Joey. I feel strangely comforted by the poem.

After a lifetime of fighting with madness and 26 years of imprisonment, Ronnie is finally free and at peace. One of the things I asked Joey, while I was interviewing him, was what made Ron special to him. Joey's a man of few words. His voice broke as he struggled to say, 'Ronnie Kray was "a Man" — and there will never be another one like him.'

Laurie O'Leary

Another person who was close to Ron and had been since Ronnie was ten years old is a man called Laurie O'Leary. The first time I met Laurie was at my wedding reception at The Hilton Hotel, Bracknell, Berkshire, in 1989. Although I had spoken to him many times on the phone, I had never actually met him in person until then. Laurie's a big man, well groomed and wears fashionable clothes that make him look younger than his years. He is a good-looking man, very friendly, but stands no nonsense from anyone. He used to be Doris Stoke's manager, and his brother Alfie was once Eric Clapton's

The Twins: Free at Last

minder. He's always been a good friend to me, too, and I love him very much. He is probably the nicest man I've ever met, a real character, and I know Laurie won't mind me saying this, but he can also talk the hind leg off a donkey!

Laurie was one of the last people to see Ron alive. He went and saw Ron on a visit two weeks before he died. Ron asked him to write a book to put the record straight about all the crap that had previously been written about him. In my opinion, Laurie O'Leary is the only person who could undertake such a task. He was with them from the age of eight. He has probably forgotten more stories about Ronnie Kray than most people could ever have known.

He knows stories from ages ago when Ronnie was a young, impetuous boy, from the time when he had tuberculosis until the day he died. He is a mine of information. Ironically enough, Reg was buried on Laurie's birthday.

Laurie has now written that book. It is called *A Man Amongst Men*. So I felt a bit apprehensive about asking him to contribute to mine. Maybe, just maybe, he might say 'No'. But Laurie is such a nice man, he had no hesitation in helping me with the information I needed. Indeed, he was only too happy to be involved. This is what he said:

The Colonel. You have to have known the man to understand him. He was a powerful man. A man that could not stand bullies. I knew him for nearly 50 years and never saw him duck away from anybody. I have read many stories in the newspapers, and I've heard mugs say that he ducked out of situations. Ronnie Kray never ducked out of fuck all. Nothing. Sure, he beat up bullies. But he wasn't a bully himself.

Only a few weeks before he died, I went to see him in the hospital. He was very ill at that time but we started chatting about this and that. Eventually the subject got around to bullies. I said, 'You hate bullies, Ron, don't you?'

Ronnie glared at me. He had completely misheard what I had said. He thought I had said that he was a bully. Quickly, I explained that I said that he hated bullies. He growled, 'Yes I do ... bastards.'

Even though he was so ill, he couldn't control his feelings towards bullies. He hated any sort of bullying, be it verbal or anything else. He always stuck up for the underdog. That was his nature.

I met Ronnie Kray when I was 10 years old, which is over 50 years ago. Ronnie was my mate, the best mate I've ever had or am ever likely to have. I lived in the next street to the twins and we all grew up together. Ronnie encouraged me to box and, at times, we used to go road running together.

We were good mates. Later on, when he had taken over a few clubs, Ronnie asked me to run this dance club for him below a casino. That was back in 1962. Then I went into running a swish club that was owned by George Harrison, one of The Beatles. They were the real days. The Swinging Sixties and, boy, did we swing.

The Twins: Free at Last

I've always been around the twins. It was fun to be around them. Dangerous, but fun. The only time I had a break from seeing Ronnie was when he was first sentenced. I didn't see him for nearly four years because villains were not allowed to visit other villains. Not that I am a villain, because I'm not. I have always been legit, but I think that the authorities thought that anyone connected with the twins at that time was a villain. It wasn't until Ronnie was transferred to Parkhurst on the Isle of Wight that I was eventually allowed to see him.

It was at Parkhurst that Ronnie became paranoid. When his mum and I visited him, he was in such a state, it was obvious he was mentally disturbed. I hardly recognised him. When he was eventually transferred to Broadmoor, I think everyone was relieved. At least in a hospital he would get the proper medication that he needed.

It was a relief, especially for his mum, Violet. She was a lovely lady. Salt of the earth. The epitome of a loving mum and, one thing's for sure, she absolutely idolised Ron.

One of the things that is not well known about Ron was his sense of humour. Without knowing it, he was an extremely funny man. It was his dry wit and one-liners that had me in tears of laughter on more than one occasion.

Years ago, I used to manage the world-famous clairvoyant called Doris Stokes. She was brilliant and just blew my mind. Ronnie was psychic himself and was very interested in seeing Doris Stokes on a visit. We made the long journey to Broadmoor to see Ronnie. As usual, he was dressed immaculately. I introduced her to him. 'Doris, this is Ronnie Kray.'

He held her hand gently and smiled. Ron was such a polite man. He took her coat and pulled the chair out for her to sit down.

'Here you are, Mrs Stokes,' he said.

It was obvious from the start that she was smitten with him.

'Oh ... you can call me Doris,' she cooed.

'Well then, you can call me Ron,' he replied. 'Would you like a pork pie or smoked salmon sandwich?'

I couldn't believe what he had just asked her. A fucking pork pie? Smoked salmon sandwich?

I think poor old Doris was in shock.

'No, I'll just have a cup of tea,' she mumbled.

Another one of Ron's visitors arrived. He was a writer and had come to talk business. We all settled down around the tea-stained table, each taking turns to talk to Ron.

Suddenly, Doris said, 'I've got your mum here with me, Ron.'

Ronnie looked at her in amazement and said, 'But Doris, my mother's dead.'

The writer and I looked at each other not knowing what to say and more importantly, trying not to laugh. Sensing my stifled laughter, Ronnie leant over and whispered in my ear, 'I think Doris should be in here, Laurie, and I should be out there.'

I could contain my laughter no longer. Both Ron

The Twins: Free at Last

and I burst out with a raucous laugh.

That day, and that visit with the writer and Doris Stokes, was a memorable one for me. We all enjoyed it so much and Doris couldn't get over what a gentleman Ron was.

The last thing Ron asked me was, 'Do you believed in life after death?'

I told him, 'Yes, I do, Ron, and you only meet nice people on the other side, not evil people.'

Ron paused, took a deep breath, dragged on his fag and smiled.

'Thank fuck for that, Laurie,' he replied.

Roy Shaw

R oy Shaw is probably the meanest-looking man I have ever seen in the whole of my life. His face, in particular his nose, looks like it's been broken more times than a bone china teacup. His cold, expressionless eyes look like they belong to a great white man-eating shark. However, this doesn't detract from his good looks. He is not very tall, about 5ft 8in, but he is as wide as he is short and always impeccably dressed. His hands are as big as a bunch of bananas with a grip like a set of Stillsons. You have never come across a smarter man than Roy Shaw.

The first time I met him was again at my wedding

The Twins: Free at Last

reception in Crowthorne, Berkshire. He was there with Joey Pyle's men. Roy was a bare-knuckle fighter. He fought Lenny McLean, another of Ron's good friends. The two champions are an awesome sight and it is impossible to tell them apart as far as strength goes.

But Roy Shaw is one mean bastard. If you cross him, you are either incredibly stupid or incredibly brave.

I phoned Roy and asked him if he wanted to be involved in the book. His response shocked me. He was really pleased that I had phoned him. He said it was an honour to be in a book about Ron. More importantly, he thought it was an honour to be one of Ron's friends.

When he first answered the telephone, he growled. I thought he had been asleep. I said, 'Sorry, Roy, were you asleep?'

'No, I always talk like this,' he said.

I laughed. So did Roy. Thank God!

Ronnie came to visit me in Broadmoor three times in all in 1963. I was doing time — a long time. Someone had told me that if you get transferred to Broadmoor it's a lot easier. You get more visits, better food, in all it's more of a relaxed régime. Better still, when the doctors think they have cured you, they send you to a normal hospital and eventually home. It's generally known that it's a quicker and simpler way of doing your time. It's called 'working your ticket'.

I was really violent. I knocked out every screw that got in my way. I did time in some of the toughest nicks in Britain. In the end, there was no place that was prepared to take me. There was only one place left — Broadmoor.

Ronnie Kray came to see me there long before he was sentenced to life. He came with Ronnie Hart, his cousin, the cousin that was later to become his betrayer. When he visited me in Broadmoor Hospital, I was having a few problems. My main problem was with my wife.

I suspected that she was messing about with another man, having an affair. Ronnie asked me if there was anything he could do. I told him about my wife. I said that I wanted the man hurt — hurt bad. Ron didn't hesitate.

'Consider it done,' he said. 'Don't worry about nothing, Roy, I'll take care of it.'

Ron came to see me a few days later. He was true to his word. Quietly he whispered, 'It's done. He's been shot.'

From that day on, I have always had the utmost respect for the man. If Ronnie Kray said that he would do something, you knew he would do it. He was a man of his word.

Jack Lee

J ack Lee doesn't look like a gangster, he looks like a bank manager. Just an ordinary, everyday man you might pass in the street without a sideways glance, but behind this ordinary 'Joe' is a hidden past spanning 30 years. There isn't anything going on in the East End that he doesn't know about; he makes it his business to know. Jack Lee is the epitome of a loveable rogue. He is full of amusing stories and anecdotes and his sense of humour is renowned. He was a good friend to Ron over the years and was extremely kind and generous to him.

This is Jack Lee's story:

The Twins: Free at Last

It was like a rugby scrum. We put our heads together. Our eyes met. Nobody said a word. Four top-ranking gang members meeting around a Formica-topped table in a hospital for the criminally insane. The meeting in Broadmoor had been called by the heads of all the different gangs that controlled London. I had never seen anything like it. Who was going to break the silence and speak first? Our eyes narrowed and we all glared at each other. It could only have been for a few seconds but seemed forever. Ron's face softened and a cheeky grin spread across his face. In an instant we all burst out laughing. Once we started laughing we couldn't stop. We went from cool professional businessmen to delinquent schoolboys. If a newspaper journalist had been a fly on the wall they would never have believed it. All four gang leaders laughing like children.

There was only one Ronnie Kray. He was such a complex character. He was probably the most genuine man I have ever met. If I took anyone to visit him, I used to pre-warn them not to compliment Ron on any of his jewellery. If they did, he would take that jewellery off and give it to them. It didn't matter what it was. Watch, cuff-links, diamond ring; if you complimented him on it, he would give it away. That's what he was like.

I have never known a man to give away as many watches as he did. But you never really knew where you stood with him. One day he would give you a five grand gold and diamond watch, the next day he would call you a 'slag and a rat'. I never took that to heart because you wasn't anyone to Ronnie Kray unless, at one time or another, he had called you a 'slag and a rat'.

I cannot say he used that phrase as a term of endearment. At the time he called you it, he fucking meant it. But that time soon passed. The following week I'd be back up on a visit, laughing and joking with him. Only Ronnie Kray had the charisma that allowed him to do that. I miss him. There will never be another man like him.

Mickey Chambers

lias 'Cornish' Mick. He is called that for the obvious reason — he comes from Cornwall. I met 'Cornish' through Joey Pyle. Whenever I went to any parties it was always Joey Pyle, Ronnie Fields and 'Cornish Mick' who escorted me. I couldn't have been in safer hands.

'Cornish' Mick is of slight build. He reminds me of a typical dad, one who would push the kids on a swing or mow the lawn on a Sunday afternoon. But 'Cornish' Mick is, without a doubt, one dangerous mother-fucker. He is a ladies' man, a real wow with the girls. His young wife, Linda, doesn't take any notice of his fraternisations. When Mick phones me he always tells me he loves me, and I hear

The Twins: Free at Last

Linda laughing in the background, saying, 'You must be talking to Kate Kray. I can hear him Kate ...'

I am proud to have Mickey 'Cornish' as my friend. He was a good friend to Ron and he is someone who would never let me down. It would not matter whose company he is in. If anybody was rude to me, 'Cornish' would stop them dead.

In this dog-eat-dog world — the underworld — sometimes you are in favour and sometimes you are not. Some are quick to jump on the band wagon and take any opportunity to slag you off. That's exactly what happened to me. Some people, some that I have never met and some I have, think that I had ulterior motives for marrying Ron. It was for money; it was for the name; it was for the fame. I've heard them all. It doesn't bother me. People are all entitled to their own opinions and when things started to go wrong between me and Ron, those same people started to slag me off, foolishly thinking they might curry favour with Ron.

They were wrong, because Ron never turned his back on me. His real friends knew that would never happen. Only the mugs thought that he would.

But at certain functions, certain people felt they knew all along that I was a 'wrong un' and had to voice their opinions. But not in 'Cornish' Mick's company they didn't.

Mick was happy be in this book. This is his story:

'Do you know Katie? Have you ever met her?'
The answers are always the same.
'No. No.'

'Then shut your foul mouth.'

I wouldn't have anyone say a bad word about Katie Kray. And I want everybody to know it. She is a good girl. If Ronnie Kray didn't marry her as quick as he did, then I would have stolen her for myself!

Not the sort of thing that anyone would say to Ronnie Kray, but I did, although I'm glad he saw the funny side of it.

We were all on a visit with him. There was Joe, Ronnie Fields, Ronnie Kray, Katie Kray and me. They hadn't been married long. We got all the relevant business out of the way and was sitting around chatting. Ron was teasing Kate, saying how at the tender age of 33 she was a little bit too old for him. Maybe he would trade her in for a new model. It was funny because he was 23 years older than her. Katie was laughing. We all were.

I turned to Ron and said, 'If you don't want her, I'll be more than happy to take her off your hands.'

The conversation stopped dead. You could have heard a pin drop. For a moment, Ron glared at me. One of those glares. Then a broad grin spread across his face. From that day, Ronnie Kray knew how I felt about his wife. She was good for him. She made him laugh. She brought happiness to him in that God-forsaken place, Broadmoor.

God knows he could do with a little happiness after being locked up for 26 years. Thirty years for the crime he committed was a diabolical liberty. In all the years I visited Ronnie Kray, I never heard him complain — not once.

'Don't worry about me. Get Reggie out.' That was his main concern. His priority was to get Reg out. But that

The Twins: Free at Last

was him. Always thinking about other people and never himself.

Tony Lambrianou

Tony Lambrianou was sentenced to life imprisonment at the Old Bailey in 1968. He stood in the dock side by side with Reg and Ron. He did 15 years for his part in disposing of Jack the Hat's body. He didn't grass. When he got life, he was 25 years old. He didn't complain — not once.

I met Tony on a visit with Ron. He is a big imposing man with silver-grey hair, looking every bit the gangster. The first thing that strikes you about Tony is his distinctive voice. It is deep and demanding. If he said 'sit', everyone would obey, not just the dog. He has a menacing look, with eyes that hold you and you would be a fool to cross him. He spent 15 years in some of the toughest prisons in Britain, and he never betrayed Ron.

Ron told me that I could always trust Tony, that he was a loyal friend. Since his release from prison, he has written a best-selling book called *Inside the Firm*. I'm glad for him. He deserves every success.

These are Tony's memories of Ron:

John Pearson approached the twins to write the book The Profession of Violence *in 1968. We had a meeting one day in Teddy Berry's pub just off Bethnal Green Road. Ronnie said that John Pearson was coming to the East End to see him and that he was going to write his autobiography. Ronnie wanted to put on a show for him and arranged for a few of the boys to be in the bar 'suited up' looking the part.*

We all sat around drinking beer, waiting for Pearson to show up. Ron was in a great mood. Half-an-hour later, John Pearson arrived. He desperately wanted to fit in with us boys. He walked in or, should I say, swaggered in. We looked at each other, then looked at him in amazement. Boy did he have some nerve. He winked at us and waved.

'All right boys?'

We laughed. So did Ron.

He got himself a drink, sat down at our table and started to talk. He liked the sound of his own voice and was going on and on about how he wanted to live in the East End, how much he loved the place and all the friendly people that lived there. What a mug. He was just trying to be one of the boys. We weren't silly. We could see straight through him. We just went along with him. Unbeknown to him, Ronnie had him sussed. He had things all lined up for the unsuspecting Mr Pearson.

Ron had a little flat just off Vallance Road. He called it the dungeon. It was a dingy little place in an old tenement building. It was a right dump — disgusting. The roof leaked and it was damp and cold. There were no carpets on the floor and an old black-and-white television stood on a wooden crate in the corner.

The wallpaper, what was left of it, looked as though it had been put up in the war. The place was running alive with cockroaches as big as armadillos. Ronnie had it as a hideaway. We used to have parties there. Drinking parties.

Ronnie laughed. 'So he wants a taste of the fucking East End does he? I'll stick him in the dungeon. That will sort him out.'

Poor old Pearson. He had to stay in that rat-hole for over a month. Worst of all, he had to pretend to Ronnie that he loved it. Ron enjoyed making him squirm. He kept asking, 'How you getting on in that flat, John?'

We all knew that he hated it. Through gritted teeth he answered every time, 'Oh, lovely, Ron. Just lovely.'

He was sick. Sick as a dog. We are talking about John Pearson. The John Pearson that wrote Ian Flemming's life story. In those days, it was a big thing to be a writer. Ronnie didn't give a fuck who he was. He wound him up mercilessly.

Pearson broke in the end. 'Do you know what, Tony?' he said. 'I hate that fucking flat.'

I'll never forget the look on his face. I didn't have the heart to tell him that Ronnie was winding him up. I bet

The Twins: Free at Last

to this day he still remembers the dungeon.

Only Ronnie Kray could get away with something like that.

I have a million stories about Ron. His sense of humour was second to none.

When Checa Berry knew that the twins were coming to drink in his pub, he would push the boat out. Anyone would think royalty was coming. He would do plates of sandwiches, have minders on the door, the whole bit. One day, I noticed that beside the till they kept a big glass jar full of little lead pellets. I called Checa over and asked him what they were.

'Fucking shotgun pellets, that's what they are,' he snapped.

He explained that his pub was shot up that often, the whole of the bar was peppered with these little lead pellets. Once they're lodged in the wall, they're a bugger to get out.'

Now and again, much to Checa's annoyance, one or two of them would work loose and fall on the floor. Every day Checa would go around muttering to himself as he picked the little pellets up and put them in the glass jar.

One night, Ronnie laughed and said, 'I don't know why he picks them up. It's a waste of time. He will be picking them up all his fucking life.'

Ronnie did like a shoot-up. He loved guns. Years later when he was in Broadmoor he still never lost his fascination for them.

I took a man into Broadmoor to visit Ronnie. His name was Bill. He came out of Romford. Like Ronnie, Bill had a thing about guns. He loved them and sold them. That was his business, or so he said.

I took him up to Broadmoor to meet Ron as I knew that they would get on. More to the point, I knew Ron would find him useful. On the visit, Bill made a fatal mistake. He told Ron that he had a Thompson sub-machine-gun and that he could get Ron any gun he wanted.

'Just say the word,' he bragged.

Ron listened intently, but said nothing. I knew he wouldn't say nothing for long.

A few days later, my phone rang. It was Ron. 'Get that Bill up on a visit again,' he said. I laughed. I knew that when Ronnie wanted to see a stranger on a second visit, it could only mean one thing. He had thought about it and had now got a use for him.

I made all the arrangements. The visit was booked for first thing the next morning. When we arrived to see Ronnie, he was dressed impeccably — as usual.

Bill and I ordered our tea from the waiter. Ron ordered his usual, non-alcoholic lager. It was obvious that he had something on his mind. We didn't have to wait long to find out what it was. He held Bill's arm and pulled him close so nobody could overhear what he was about to say.

'When I get out,' he whispered, 'can I loan your machine-gun? You see, I still have some unfinished business.'

Bill was stunned. He didn't know what to say. He had visited Ronnie acting the big man. Talking big. To Bill it was just a fantasy. To Ronnie it was stark reality.

The Twins: Free at Last

Ron said to me once, 'Never forget what they did to us. Never trust anyone.'

By that, he meant the bastards that betrayed us. I will never forget those words from Ronnie. They are wise words. He made the mistake of trusting certain people and it got him 30 years. Me, too. I trusted the same people and got 15 years. I, too, will never forget what they did to us. To use Ronnie Kray's own words, they are 'slags and rats'. You have to respect the man. Ronnie Kray demanded respect.

I always came away from Broadmoor after visiting Ron feeling very depressed. The reason was, I always used to tell Ronnie that, one day, he would be free. I wanted to believe that, but in my heart I knew that was never going to happen.

We were all sentenced at the Old Bailey together. I did 15 years. I was the first one of the lifers to get out. Ronnie Kray was delighted. He was genuinely delighted. In the 26 years that Ron spent in prison I never heard him complain. I also never heard him talk about being free. I found that sad.

Albert Reading

I met Albert Reading on a secret rendezvous on the South Circular in a shop called The World of Leather. Ron had asked me to ring Albert to arrange a meeting with him to discuss some business they were doing at the time. I didn't know what he looked like or how I was going to recognise him, but that was not a problem as I had been in that position many times before. I walked into that shop on a Saturday afternoon not fully prepared for what was going to happen.

I looked around the half-empty shop, carefully studying potential buyers. There was a fat man wearing a

The Twins: Free at Last

pair of striped shorts. He had a small child on his shoulders who was eating an ice cream. Nah ... that wasn't him. A yuppie brushed past me wearing a cheap suit and holding a filofax, talking on his mobile phone. Nah ... that wasn't him either.

I stood in the middle of the shop gazing around; the smell of the leather was overwhelming. I wondered where the hell he was. Then, from out of nowhere, a swivel chair spun round. The man in the chair was striking. He wore a silver-grey suit with a tightly knotted silk tie. His rugged face was tanned, and his jet-black hair, slightly greying at the sides, gave him a distinguished look. He oozed money, power and sex appeal. It was Albert Reading.

He leaned back in the chair nonchalantly, seemingly without a care for anyone or anything. He smiled. I remember thinking how handsome he was, a very distinctive man, his appearance giving nothing away about his chequered past.

Albert has spent 36 years in prison, his last sentence was a 25-year stretch for armed robbery. He has had the birch. He has been stabbed, shot, beaten, but he is the most personable and generous man you could wish to meet. Instantly, we clicked.

This is Albert Reading's story:

I met the twins in Stepney, initially through boxing. My dad was a professional fighter and the twins used to visit him — he would talk to them about boxing for hours. We were all called up to the Army together and were billeted to Colchester barracks. The Sergeant Major took an instant dislike to us. He thought he could shout at us and order us about. He was wrong. He was soon to experience the wrath of Ronnie Kray.

When the post was distributed, the Sergeant Major yelled out your name.

'... Reading ... Kray ...'

If there was a letter for you, he tossed it at you like skimming a pebble across a pond. This particular day, Ronnie received a letter from his mother.

'Kray,' the Sergeant Major yelled, then he skimmed the letter in Ron's direction.

The letter flew through the air as if in slow motion and landed in front of Ronnie's shiny boots. Ron's eyes narrowed. He looked straight into the Sergeant Major's eyes. Every one of us knew that look. It was the look of trouble. Ron motioned to the letter on the floor.

'Pick it up,' he growled.

For someone to speak to the Sergeant Major in such a manner was unheard of.

'Pick my mother's letter up,' Ron whispered again.

The Sergeant Major looked dumbfounded, but stood his ground and bellowed, 'You what, you 'orrible little man?'

Ron's eyes were as black as thunder. He glared at the Sergeant Major. 'You heard what I said. Pick it up.'

Ron never raised his voice. He never took his eyes off his adversary. Their eyes were locked and it was a battle of wills. There was no way Ron was going to back down; his face said it all. The Sergeant Major sensed trouble — big trouble. He looked away from Ron's piercing gaze.

The Twins: Free at Last

Slowly, not making any sudden moves, he bent down and picked up the letter and submissively handed it to Ron.

For his insolence, Ron was sent to the choky, but it didn't bother him — he was a man of principle. If he felt strongly enough about something, the consequences were irrelevant. I loved Ron's ways, his manner. He wasn't mouthy, he was a man of his word. I had the utmost respect for him.

Main picture: It is a little known fact that Reg was allowed to visit Ron every three months. I would arrange a seafood lunch for them – this is a picture of what the Broadmoor chef would prepare.

Right: This badge was made 22 years after Reg was sent away; it took another 11 years for him to be released.

22 YEARS
ENOUGH IS ENOUGH
FREE REGGIE KRAY

Top: The gravestone of Ron and Reg's beloved parents, Violet and Charles.

Below: The impressive sight of the floral tributes at Ron's funeral. Reg's tribute reads, 'To the Other Half of Me'.

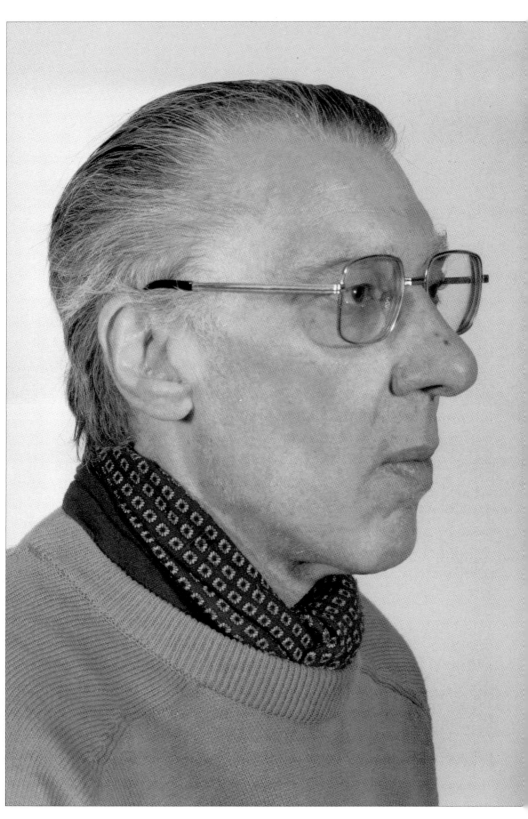

The last picture ever taken of Ron.

Top: Notorious underworld name Frankie Fraser arrives to pay his respects at Reg's funeral.

Below: One of the floral tributes to Reg.

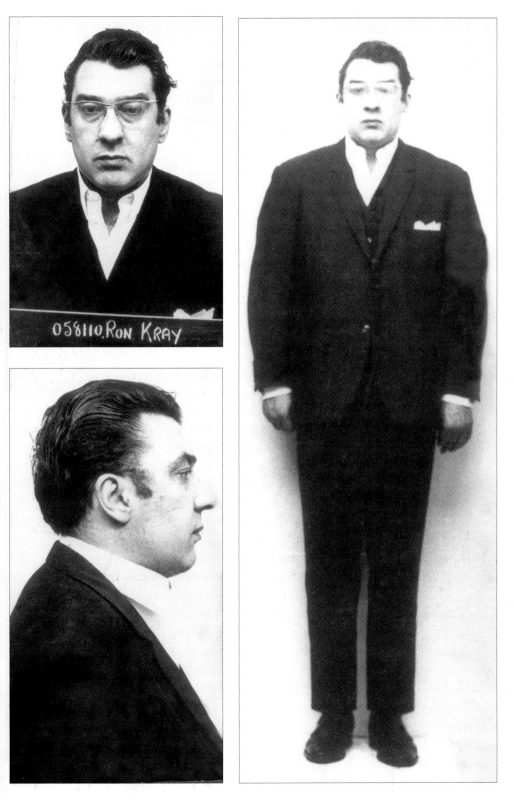

Mugshots of Ron Kray, taken after the twins' arrest in 1968 for the murders of George Cornell and Jack 'The Hat' McVitie.

Ron and Reg with their snakes Nipper and Gerrard, named after the two policemen that were pursuing them. David Bailey took the picture and said of the twins, 'Reg was always charming but I found Ron a bit scary.'

058111 REG. KRAY.

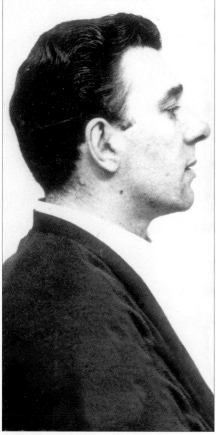

Reg's mugshots after the big arrest in 1968.

Billy Murray

R on loved the showbiz world. Even as a kid he appeared in a film called *The Magic Box*, and in later years he surrounded himself by people from the film world – Barbara Windsor, George Sewell, and a young man called Billy Murray.

Billy is an actor — a bloody good actor, too. He has been in many films and in countless TV programmes. At present, he is in the popular Thames Television programme *The Bill*, in which he plays DS Don Beech.

Ron phoned me and wanted to see me on a visit urgently. There was nothing unusual in that. He always wanted to see me and it was always urgent. As usual, I made the long journey to Broadmoor. Ron was waiting for me. He always looked smart, but on this particular day he was dressed immaculately.

We sat down at the small table in the crowded visiting hall. Ron explained that he was expecting another visitor, a special visitor. His name was Billy Murray.

'You'll like Billy,' Ron smirked. 'You wait 'til you see him, he's handsome.'

Ron has said that before but his idea of handsome was certainly not mine. So I just smiled sweetly at him and nodded.

Ron didn't take a blind bit of notice of me as he was far too busy talking about Billy. He went on to say that a few of The Firm went to Barcelona back in the 1960s and Billy went with them.

'Was he one of your boys?' I asked.

Ron smiled. 'Well,' he said, 'Bill was the only one who got away.' But he wouldn't tell me any more. He told me that he'd put Billy through acting college – that's how close they were.

But later he also told me, 'You'd be surprised ... the "faces" that didn't get away from me, but some secrets are best left untold.'

However, on this occasion, I had to agree with Ron. Billy Murray is indeed handsome.

It didn't make any difference to Ron that Billy never became one of his boys because he thought Billy was a really nice person, and if he couldn't have him as one of his boys then he wanted him as a friend. That was back in the 1960s. They remained friends until the day Ron died in 1995.

Harry Roberts

In 1965, Harry Roberts was Britain's most wanted man. On Friday, 12 August, in a quiet street near London's Shepherd's Bush, he and two accomplices gunned down three policemen.

Until then, the murder of a British policeman was virtually unheard of. To most people, it was the kind of thing you only saw in Hollywood gangster movies. The crime, and the front-page photographs of three bloodied policemen lying dead in the street, shocked the country.

Two of the killers — John Duddy and Jack Whitney — were arrested within a week, but it was three long months before the police caught up with Harry Roberts.

In 1966, at the end of his trial, Mr Justice Glynn Jones described the murders as 'perhaps the most heinous crimes to have been committed in this country for a generation or more.' He sent Harry Roberts to prision for life with a recommendation that he serve at least 30 years.

I first met Harry in Gartree High Security Prison in the late 1980s. By then he had served over 20 years. Later, I wrote Harry's story in my book *Natural Born Killers*. It was the first time he had told his story to anyone. Since then we have become friends, and he phones me from prision every week.

I asked him if he wanted to contribute to this book, and he was more than happy to give his opinion of Ron. In the next post I received a letter from Harry. His letters are always beautifully written. I have not changed a single word, and this is what Harry Roberts said about Ronnie Kray:

I first knew of Ron and Reg Kray when I was 17. They were a few years older than me, so we were just acquaintances. As the years went by, I used to see them in the night clubs and restaurants around London.

I got to know Ronnie well when we were both locked up in the Special Security Block of Parkhurst Prison.

Ron was a really good guy. He treated everyone with respect and he expected to be treated with respect in return. Ron was always helping people. If he knew someone did not have the money for a visit from their family, he would make sure they got a visit or toys for the kids at Christmas. If he saw someone was short of a pair of weight-lifting boots, they would get a pair of weight-lifting boots. You could always rely on Ron to keep his word — if he said something was 'sorted', it was sorted.

Lenny McLean

enny McLean is, without doubt, the 'Guv'nor'. His bestselling book *The Guv'nor* made him the most famous hard man ever. He was awesome – big, massive, standing at well over 6ft.

Lenny was a bare-knuckle fighter — the best, not only in this country, but in the States as well. He went to the USA and beat the Mafia bare-knuckle champion. He won $30,000 in one night. He was due to go back to his hotel room after the fight, but changed his mind and went directly to the airport as a precaution. Anything could have happened; gunmen waiting in the lobby or unwelcome

The Twins: Free at Last

visitors in the middle of the night, but Lenny was too cute for that. Nobody, including the Mafia, was going to take that $30,000 from him.

Lenny McLean's reputation preceded him, inevitably reaching Ronnie Kray in Broadmoor. Ronnie told me once that he had never met a tougher man than Lenny McLean. But that's not what really makes Lenny dangerous. Being tough is one thing; being tough and having a brain is another. Lenny was very intelligent — sharp as a tack. He was aware of everything going on around him, and even when talking, he studied every move, every look and every gesture. I suppose he had to in his profession — the business of violence. But he used this quality in a constructive rather than a destructive way, becoming an actor. His most famous film was *Lock, Stock and Two Smoking Barrels*, but he was also in films with Bruce Willis and has appeared in the TV programme *The Knock* and countless other shows.

Lots of people have had a pop at Lenny. He was stabbed on numerous occasions, and even shot, but was rarely confronted face to face, because if you messed with Lenny, you were messing with the best.

I visited Lenny at his home on the outskirts of London before he died of cancer in 1998, and asked him how remembered Ron:

Ronnie Kray was not brash or loud, although the media portrayed him that way. On the contrary, I found him quiet and humble, which surprised me. Ron's appearance was always very smart — his suits, his shoes, in fact, his whole presence, was overwhelming. The perfect gentleman. I was proud to be Ronnie Kray's friend.

And I know that Ronnie was proud to have known Lenny McLean, too.

RON ON DEATH

I'm not frightened of dying. Strangely enough, I believe in the death penalty. In fact, I think it would have been kinder to hang me. It certainly would have been quicker. Sometimes, in Broadmoor, the days are long and the nights an eternity.

Being locked away for 30 years is a slow, drawn-out way to spend your life – my life. But I don't regret the crimes I committed. I don't regret anything about my life – only getting caught. I never want anyone to apologise for me, because I'm not sorry. Many have stood in judgement over me. But there is only one judge – God.

THE END
OF AN ERA

In March 1995, I got a phonecall saying that Ron was seriously ill. He had been taken to Wexham Park Hospital in Slough, suffering from a heart-attack. He was 61 years old and had served 27 years of his 30-year prison sentence, most of it in Broadmoor. When I received the phonecall, I knew that Ron must be very ill for the authorities to take him out of Broadmoor to an outside hospital.

The caller was frantic. He wanted to tell me exactly what had happened. Ron had got up in the morning, and washed and dressed as normal. The nurse unlocked his cell door. Ron asked the nurse for a light for his first cigarette of the day. Patients are not allowed matches or a lighter because of the dangerous arsonists that are housed there, which is a reasonable precaution given the circumstances. Down one side of the corridor, built into the walls, are special bricks for the nurses to strike a match against. Nurses are the only ones allowed to carry the matches — minus the box. Broadmoor rules state that the matches and the box are not to be kept together at any time in case they are stolen.

Ron took a long drag from his cigarette and stepped out of his room, he was happy enough. He started to walk along the corridor towards the day-room, even stopping to pass the time of day with another patient. Suddenly, he stumbled and fell against the wall, gasping for breath. He clutched his chest and the colour drained from his face.

Realising there was a problem, the other patient raised the alarm by shouting for help. Two nurses rushed to Ron's aid. He had stopped breathing. Anxiously, they tried to revive him. Someone shouted, 'Get a fucking ambulance.'

Inmates rushed from their cells, and the whisper went round: 'Ronnie Kray's collapsed.' The chances are that the newspapers would get hold of the story quicker than Ron would get to the hospital.

Getting an ambulance for such a high-profile prisoner is not as simple as it sounds. The authorities have to take into consideration the fact that it might be an elaborate hoax. Police and security are put on red alert. Broadmoor goes on 'lock down'. All movement inside the hospital grinds to a halt. They can't take any chances.

Back on the ward, inmates were quickly head-counted back into their cells before the ambulance was allowed to reverse up to the door. Eventually, Ron was put in the back of the ambulance. He was covered in a red blanket with an oxygen mask on his face.

Broadmoor's huge wooden gates were flung open and the ambulance swept through, sirens wailing and blue lights flashing. A helicopter hovered above the ambulance as it sped down the narrow streets. Road blocks were set up quickly and the surrounding motorways were sealed off; the security could not have been tighter even for the President of the United States. Police outriders on their motorbikes escorted the ambulance to the hospital. Inside the ambulance, paramedics were frantically working on Ron.

Doug, who was a nurse at Broadmoor, phoned me. His voice broke, and although clearly upset, he told me not to worry and not to bother going to the hospital as the security was watertight. Nobody was allowed to see Ron, not even me.

On the practical side, I knew they must have whisked Ron out of Broadmoor with no personal effects of his own. No pyjamas, no Brylcreem, no cigarettes, absolutely nothing, not even a toothbrush. As usual, all his belongings would be left behind. These personal things were as important to Ronnie as you and me. There was no one else to get them, so I decided to go into town to buy what he needed and take them to him, not necessarily to see him, just to leave him the bits at the hospital with a note. I drove into Maidstone town centre. I nipped into Marks and Spencer's and bought him a

The Twins: Free at Last

couple of vests and a new pair of pyjamas. There was a long queue at the checkout. Anxiously, I waited to be served. It seemed like everybody wanted to pay by cheque. I was in a hurry because I wanted to get to Slough before the M25 got too busy and I still had to go home and change my clothes.

Eventually I was served, and raced home to get changed. Then it dawned on me that I had forgotten his Brylcreem. Ron was so particular he always used Brylcreem. So I stopped off at a local Spar shop to buy some. As I was walking around the shop I could hear the radio gently playing in the background. Suddenly, there was a news-flash saying, 'We interrupt this broadcast with news just in. The gangster, Ronnie Kray, is dead.'

I went numb. I did not know what to do. Ronnie. Dead? It couldn't be. They must have got it wrong. I dropped my wire shopping basket on the floor and leant against the shelves. The lady who owned the shop approached me. She knew who I was. She had a look on her face, that look of awkwardness and pity.

'I am so sorry to hear about your sad loss ...'

I couldn't speak. I burst into tears and ran from the shop. My mind was racing. I had to get to a phone.

As I walked into my house, I could hear my phone ringing. In actual fact, it never stopped ringing. Mostly it was the Press, all wanting to know the ins and outs of Ronnie's death. Others were Ron's friends desperate for news. I just did not know what to do. So I rang Maidstone prison where Reggie is and left a message with them saying who I was and my home phone number. I wanted to speak to him. I needed to speak to him. A friend intercepted all my calls because I was too distressed even to be polite to the many callers all wanting to send their condolences.

Half-an-hour later, Reggie managed to get through to me and he was inconsolable. We both were. Each sobbing uncontrollably, unable to speak to each other. Through the sobs, I told Reggie that I would be going away for a couple of days. I had to. I wanted to think. I wanted to be alone. He agreed it was a good idea that I went away and didn't speak to the Press. Reggie was in prison so the Press couldn't get to him. Nobody was able to phone him either so, in a way, he was shielded from the frenzy of activity. I looked out of my window and saw the Press beginning to gather.

With the help of a friend, I gathered up a few belongings and got into my car, despite the Press, and went to Brighton for a couple of days. I walked along the sea-front on my own, desperately trying to gather my thoughts.

I think he knew that he was going to die. He had put all his affairs in order. I hadn't heard from him for two weeks, since he sent me flowers. I wandered along the sea-front feeling empty. I couldn't get Ron out of my mind.

I returned home to the Press onslaught and the endless phonecalls from Ron's friends all wanting details of the funeral. When? Where? Time? Place? All questions I couldn't answer yet. I phoned Broadmoor to see if I needed to make any arrangements. They said that Reggie had it all under control.

Two days before his 'state' funeral through London's East End, I slipped quietly into the Chapel of Rest. I was dressed in the pin-striped suit that Ron had always admired, and my eyes were shielded by Jackie O-style glasses. I took a huge wreath of white carnations and red roses with me shaped like a broken heart. I had come to say my private goodbyes to my husband.

I drove my small car through Bethnal Green. Market traders lined the street, plying their goods as usual; their cockney accents booming over the rush-hour traffic, the banter of the EastEnders never changing. 'Git yer luvly narnas 'ere.' Life goes on.

As I approached the Chapel of Rest, I noticed a wall of photographers who had been cordoned off, opposite the entrance to the chapel. Outside stood sullen-faced security men, hands deep inside their dark overcoat pockets, all looking like the robbers' dog. I parked my car around the side of the building. Four minders were waiting for me.

Avoiding the Press cameras, they smuggled me through a side entrance and showed me into the room where Ron's body was laid out. There was a strange smell in the air, vaguely clinical, like a hospital. I will never forget that awful smell, the smell of death, it made such an impact on me. The room was cold. I shivered.

I'd never seen a dead body before and, at first, I was frightened to go up to the coffin. I took a deep breath. I pulled up a chair and sat on Ron's right side — by his good ear. He looked peaceful, but he didn't look like Ron. He had all this make-up on and he wouldn't have liked that, so I got a big bundle of tissues out of my bag and gently wiped some of it off.

Nervously, I pushed the lid of the coffin down so that I could see his hands — I always loved his hands. They were strong, masculine hands with short nails that were always scrupulously clean. Ron always said you can tell a man by his handshake. A firm handshake meant a trustworthy man.

I got out the cigarettes I'd brought with me — ten John Player Specials. Only ten because, still in my heart, I wanted him to give up smoking, knowing it was bad for him. I unwrapped the cellophane and put them in the coffin close to his right hand, within easy reach. That's what he wanted. 'Kate,' he had said, 'when I die, make sure I've got some fags with me so I can smoke them on the way to Heaven.'

I was scared to touch him at first, so I stroked his hair. They'd parted it all wrong and it wasn't Brylcreemed — Ron always liked his hair Brylcreemed. I wanted to go and get some, but I thought I had better not, so I rearranged it. I remember thinking that at least they had put his teeth in, because his face wasn't sunken. The room was filled with lovely spring flowers.

It was cool and calm and there were crucifixes on the wall, which made the memories flood back. Ron was very religious. I remember him telling me once to get him a gold cross and chain.

'And make sure you get me one with a little man on it,' he said.

The Twins: Free at Last

He did make me laugh sometimes.

In the chapel, I didn't know what to say at first, because it was all so odd. I had lost my voice and was whispering away, so I tried to keep close to his good ear so he could hear me.

I said, 'You'd laugh if you could see all the palaver that's going on ... everyone is very upset and they are all arguing about who's going to carry your coffin.'

Once I had started talking, it became a lot easier. I sat talking to Ron for a hour. I had a lot to talk about. I told him how everyone was driving me mad. The world and his wife wanted to come to the funeral. It was pandemonium.

It was turning into a four-ringed circus. We certainly had a strong-man or two. How he would have loved all the fuss.

He often spoke of his funeral and he said he wanted to be buried the old-fashioned way, with the horses wearing plumes pulling a glass hearse. I told him I'd make sure he got what he wanted and I'd see that there was 'The Colonel' — his nickname — spelled out in chrysanthemums along the side of the hearse. He said 'smashin''.

I like to remember him on the good visits we had — him saying, 'Come on, me old Dutch, you sit by me!' And sitting outside in the summer with his shirt off, laughing. Now he was dead, cold in his coffin. I started to cry. There was no white hankie, there was no comfort, but what happened next made me laugh.

The End of an Era

Workmen outside of the Chapel of Rest were repairing a window. I could hear them in the background, whistling, hammering, getting on with their job. Life goes on. I was distraught. Out of the blue, one of the workmen yelled, 'Where's me fucking hammer?'

I looked at Ron and laughed. Even in death he knew the precise moment for humour. Laughter had been so important in our relationship. Against all odds, what was often called Britain's most bizarre marriage had lasted longer than five years.

So many people wanted to attend Ron's funeral that the arrangements were not going to be simple. On the day of the funeral, I was ill with the 'flu and bronchitis. My publisher's brother, David Blake, sent his stretch limo with blacked out windows and a chauffeur for my use for the day.

The question was, who was going to be my minder? Not wanting to upset anyone was hard, so I said 'Yes' to them all. There was Harry 'H' and Albert Reading in the limo. Waiting outside the church was 'Cornish' Mick and Ronnie Fields.

The arrangements were very carefully done for the funeral by a lovely lady called Flanagan, a long-term friend of the twins. Flanagan was the first Page Three girl. She is a blond bombshell even in her early 50s with a heart of gold.

On the day of Ron's funeral, it seemed that the whole of London came to a standstill. It was later described by film director Michael Winner as 'a great spectacle, equal to the Coronation or the Lord's Mayor

The Twins: Free at Last

Show.' It was heralded as the biggest funeral the country had seen since former Prime Minister Sir Winston Churchill's in 1965, when an estimated 50,000 people turned out to pay their respects.

The service was held in St Matthew's Church, Bethnal Green, and led by Father Christopher Bedford, on Wednesday, 29 March 1995 at noon.

I arrived at the Church to be greeted by a sea of Press from all over the world. The limo pulled up in front of the gates and I stepped out to be greeted by the minders.

On the instructions of Reg, no one was allowed into the church until he had arrived because he wanted to be the first to go into the church to say his goodbyes.

When he arrived, it was complete pandemonium. He stepped from the car still handcuffed to his guards. The crowd went wild. Everyone was pushing and shoving trying to get a glimpse of him. He looked tiny compared to his guards. He tried to raise his arm to wave to the crowd, but one of the officers pulled it down. Quickly, he was whisked around to the back entrance of the church.

I looked through the glass door at the entrance of the church. I saw the saddest sight I am ever likely to see. It was Reggie Kray standing beside the coffin of his beloved twin, his head bowed, his face expressionless. He just stared at the oak coffin. He looked so alone. I wanted to break down the door and put my arms around him, just to comfort and hold him. My heart went out to him. A million thoughts must have been running through his mind. Who would he write to? Who would he argue with? Who would he love? What would he do without Ronnie? Poor Reg, I thought, how was he going to cope? He stood beside the coffin for what seemed an eternity.

Flanagan broke my thoughts as she unlocked the door. Reggie stood beside her with an outstretched hand. He shook every man's hand and kissed every lady. Reggie was very strong; he held me tight. I sobbed. He whispered in my ear. 'Now's not the time for tears — we cry later.' He gave me his hankie and nodded his head. Just hearing his voice made me worse — he sounded just like Ron.

Flanagan showed us to our allocated seats and we all had our own service sheets with our names on them. The church was full to capacity. Flanagan had to lock the door to prevent anyone else getting in.

Needless to say, the service was very emotional but all the time I was trying to stifle my cough with lozenges and nasal sprays. A video camera panned about, zooming in for close-ups of our reactions. I found it very intrusive. Some bright spark decided it would make a good video. Even in death they wouldn't leave Ron alone. Was nothing sacred?

My thoughts went back to when I went to pay my last respects to Ron in the Chapel of Rest. My last words to him were, 'If I was organising your funeral, I would have played the song "I Will Always Love You" by Whitney Houston.'

Nobody was in the room when I said that. Nobody except Ron, of course. He hated that sort of music. He preferred classical music, his favourite being *Madam Butterfly*.

The funeral service continued; it was beautiful. Frank Sinatra sang 'My Way'. A list of names was read out of friends who were unavoidably detained, friends from Broadmoor and prisons all around the country. The hymn 'Morning Has Broken' was sung by the choir.

There was a deafening silence while a message was read out by a friend from Reggie. 'My brother Ron is now free and at peace. Ron had great humour, a vicious temper, and was kind and generous. He did it all his way but, above all, he was a man, that is how I will always remember my twin brother Ron.

'We wish for only good to come from Ron's passing away and what is about to follow is our tribute to Ron. It is a symbol of peace in that the four pall bearers will be Charlie Kray, Freddie Forman, Johnny Nash and Teddy Dennis; each one represents an area of London, North, South, East and West.'

They all encircled Ron's coffin in a minutes' silence.

Another hymn, 'Fight The Good Fight', was sung by the choir. Each of the hymns was chosen carefully and was relevant to Ron's life.

A beautiful poem was then read, one that I will always remember:

> *Do not stand at my grave and weep*
> *I am not there. I do not sleep.*
> *I am a thousand winds that blow.*

The End of an Era

I am the diamond glints on snow.
I am the sunlight on ripened grain,
I am the gentle autumn rain.
When you awaken in the morning's hush
I am the swift uplifting rush
Of quiet birds in circled flight.
I am the soft stars that shine at night.
Do not stand at my grave and cry,
I am not there; I did not die.

Up to that point, I had been trying to contain my coughing and breathing difficulties due to my bronchitis. I hadn't even looked at the service sheet. Right at the end, unbeknown to me, 'I Will Always Love You' was played and I could not contain my grief any longer. I howled, not quite believing it. Of all the songs they could have chosen, they chose that one, the one that I had told Ron about in the privacy of the Chapel of Rest.

Every gangster in the church pulled out a white handkerchief as they shed a tear. The service finished and we were ready to leave. I put my dark glasses on to hide my puffy eyes. But nothing could hide my nose; it was bigger than my hat and must have been the first bit of me to leave the church.

There were funeral cars as far as the eye could see. Ronnie's coffin was in a Victorian glass hearse drawn by six black, plumed horses. Completely taking up one side of the hearse was Reggie's floral tribute. It read: 'The other half of me'.

It was magnificent. The funeral cortège of flower-

The Twins: Free at Last

decked black limos followed directly behind the horse-drawn hearse. Reggie was in the first car. He sat in the back with two obligatory prison officers. Thousands of people from all over the world attended. There were sightseers on rooftops, and some had shimmied up lampposts to get a better view. The streets were lined as far as the eye could see.

Reg sat in the back of the car alone, no family or friends to comfort him in his hour of need. No compassion was shown by the authorities allowing Reg to be accompanied by someone who cared.

Behind Reg's car was Charlie Kray's. Behind Charlie's was mine. On top of every car were floral tributes. Mine was a big red heart trimmed in white carnations, but I had asked the florist to tear it in half so that it resembled my broken heart. On my card I wrote, 'Tears in my eyes I can wipe away, but the pain in my heart will always stay.'

After the church service in Bethnal Green, the cortège wound its way through the East End on a two-hour journey to the cemetery in Chingford. Ron was to be buried next to his mum and dad.

There were thousands of floral tributes, including a wreath of orchids from Ronnie's friend of 30 years, *EastEnders* actress Barbara Windsor; an R-shaped wreath from singer Morrissey, who had written a song about the Krays; and a wreath from The Who's Roger Daltrey. Mourners included *EastEnders* star Patsy Palmer and Helen Keating from TV's *London's Burning*. Mourners came from every spectrum of society, from dustmen to pop singers. All had come to pay their respects to 'The Colonel'. Some had come out of curiosity.

During the journey, women were banging on the windows of the passing cortège, men were crying openly. TV crews were trying to stick their cameras in the windows of the passing limos. Some journalists were talking Chinese, some were talking with Australian accents. An entrepreneur was selling 'FREE REGGIE KRAY' T-shirts. I will never forget it.

Eventually, the cortège arrived at the graveyard. Again, it was totally surrounded by a security cordon. Immediate family were whisked to the open grave.

Unbeknown to me, there were armed commandos positioned in the graveyard to watch my back. I heard a noise directly behind me and I turned around. The familiar face of Bobby Wren appeared from behind a gravestone with camouflage marks on his cheeks. But this was no ordinary GI Joe, and certainly no mug. Bobby is a bit of a handful, and likes to keep a low profile. He winked at me; he meant business.

We stood around the open grave. The coffin was lowered. The vicar began to commit Ron's body to the ground.

'Earth to earth, ashes to ashes, dust to dust.'

I kissed my hand and touched the coffin as it was lowered into the ground.

Ron often talked about his death. He wasn't frightened of dying, and sometimes I think he even looked forward to it. He often told me that only God could judge him. When he wrote his poems, a lot of

The Twins: Free at Last

them were about dying. These two are my favourites. The first one is called 'The Troubled Mind'. I think that when Ron wrote this, he was talking about himself. It's about the hopeless souls which are trapped inside the criminally insane person's mind. I'll let you judge for yourself.

> As I walk along the Broadmoor corridors
> I see my fellow man, trudging the floors
> Getting nowhere, like a boat with no oars.
> They all have a troubled mind
> Most are looking for the peace of mind
> They cannot find.
> Some are cruel, some are kind
> God forgive them who have the troubled mind;
> Only when they go to The Great Beyond,
> peace will they find.

This second poem is called *Peace of Mind*. I asked Ron once that, if he could have one wish, what it would be. I thought his answer would be freedom, wealth, or a chance to start again to alter the outcome of his prison sentence. But no, it was none of these things.

Ron paused for a moment to think. He took a drag on his cigarette, and lent back in his chair. I looked at him. His craggy face looked tired. He sighed and said, 'If I had one wish, it would be peace of mind.'

A few days later, in the post I received this beautiful poem. I think that visit and my question prompted this poem.

The End of an Era

As I ask for peace of mind
And think of the sheep on the green hills
And try to combat my mixed-up wills
I, of God, ask for peace of mind.
That, only when I take the big sleep, will I find
No man knows me
Only He can my mind see
And with the big sleep, set me free.

I honestly believe that Reggie never recovered from the shock of his brother's death. Two years after Ron passed away he married a lady called Roberta – after thirty years in prison maybe that's just what he needed. But his health went downhill fast – Ron and Reg were two halves of the same person, and when Ron died he lost the will to live.

In August 2000 he was taken from HMP Wayland to hospital suffering from a suspected kidney infection. It soon transpired that it was cancer. And so, after 30 years inside, the Home Secretary Jack Straw released him on compassionate grounds. Was that an act of kindness? To say to a dying man, you're free to go – this is what you've missed for 30 years, and now you'll never have it. It doesn't seem it to me; Reg should have been released years ago.

He moved to the Norfolk and Norwich hospital. Reg was a born fighter, but even freedom could not help him in this final battle. The cancer was inoperable, and treatment was withdrawn. On Thursday 20th September,

The Twins: Free at Last

Reg was allowed home to die.

On Sunday, 1 October, Joey Pyle, Freddie Foreman, Johnny Nash and other gangsters congregated at Reg's bedside. They knew that today was going to be the day that the legend of the Krays would become exactly that – a legend. The end of an era.

Reg had been drifting in and out of consciousness for a few days. The chaps around his bed weren't sure if he could hear them, but he was breathing heavily. The last of the Krays was clearly in pain. Freddie Foreman put his hand on his head and said, 'Let go, let go Reg. Just let go, old son.' They all knew that this was the one battle that Reggie Kray couldn't win – try though he might.

A couple of breaths later he was dead.

Wednesday 11th October saw the burial of the final Kray. Reg's funeral was everything it was expected to be – the East End did him proud, just as it did Ron. As I watched the cortège slow down along Vallance Road, the twins' childhood home, a whole load of thoughts went through my head. I thought of the times I spent in Broadmoor and Gartree, visiting with the twins, and I thought of the wasted years they spent behind bars. I thought of how Ron needed Reg; and of how Reg lost his will to live after Ron passed away. It was a sad day, but somehow I couldn't feel too sad, because I knew that at last they were together again, and that is all they ever wanted. Reg's floral tribute to Ron had read 'To the Other Half of Me'. Ron and Reg were two halves of the same person. Now they had been joined again. And the

The End of an Era

flowers on Reg's hearse that day said it all: 'Free At Last'.

All these thoughts went through my head. But most of all, I thought to myself, Look out heaven – the Kray twins are on their way ...

RON AND REG
IN THEIR
OWN WORDS

During the time I knew them, Reg and Ron sent me literally hundreds upon hundreds of letters. Some of them contained very everyday comments and requests; some of them were rather more interesting.

This is a selection of some of those letters…

25th APRIL 1991 Monday

① Don't care all the
project business
should be over by
the end of next week
so if it is ok
— will make a
nice bit of cash

So keep cheerful
— are going
to be ok so
don't worry

As soon as I get
some cash
I'll make sure I
am scar...
back to home
xmas to the
final calls
to me of a
night

God bless
love
Tom
Ron
xxxxxx

25th April 1991 – Ron Kray

Dear Kate

All the project Business should be done by the end of next
week. So if it is OK you will have a nice bit of cash.

So keep cheerful, you are going to be OK So don't worry.

PTO

As soon as I have some cash you will have some. I am glad
you got the flower.

Thanks for the phone calls to me of a night.

God bless
Love from
Ron

12TH MAY   MONDAY

O MY DEAR WIFE KATE
I AM VERY SORRY ABOUT
TODAY, I HOPE — ARE OK.

        I HOPE — WILL COME
   TO SEE ME   ON
        THURSDAY AFTERNOON

        I THINK — WORLD OF
              — — —

X X   XX —
  XX
   X X   GOD BLESS
   X XXX   XX   LOVE
                         FROM
   P.T.O.   XXXXXX...

KATE THANKS FOR PICKING
   ME UP TO NIGHT.
I WAS HAPPY WITH —
   DAD,
   I DON'T DESERVE
   SOME ONE AS
   NICE AS —

        — LOOKED
          BEAUTIFUL
          TODAY

        I LOVE — A LOT

        — WAS

   OUR WEDDING
   AS — MEAN —

12th May – Ron Kray

My dear wife Kate

I am very sorry about today. I hope you are OK

I hope you will come to see me on Thursday afternoon.

I think the world of you – you know that.

God bless
Love from
Ron

PTO

Thanks for phoning me up tonight
I was happy when you did.
I don't deserve someone as nice as you.
You looked beautiful today.
I love you a lot. I won't ever have a go at you again.

xxxx

14th MAY SUNDAY   Monday

① DEAR KATE I hope — are

      OK Some flowers are

      on the way

          keep your chin up

              — will be

          OK I love

          xxx

              Coll Brill love

                  to

                  Ron

                  x x x x
                  x x x x
                  x x x x
                  x x x x
                  x x x x
                      x x

14th May, Sunday – Ron Kray

Dear Kate

I hope you are OK. Some flowers are on the way
Keep your chin up.

You will be OK. I know this.

God bless
Love from
Ron

Kate,

I've BEEN A while
I like I am I
Cant not SlEEP.

I would like you or you all
ACCept time ans
not with other PEOPLE.

I would also Influence you
to get Gaba ain ans
I would like also to
Come to this tribe
so. el we can go
with me ans we
who have who

Chance of actual out ceethate.
But you look back all how
who you see many ans
women a only each of this
cult normalize an give
over to you too.
I've at a Bristt
I dont want who
cons ann a million
like you look.
Yours

Reg Kray, Lewes Prison
Lewes
Sussex

31st May Wednesday 5am

Kate,

I've been awake since 1am, I could not sleep.
You should see Ron on your own all the time and not with other people.
You should also influence Ron to get fresh air and sunshine, also to come to this prison so as he can be with me, and he will have more chance of getting out eventually.
Put your foot down all round.

Will you send Percy and Warren a copy each of the 'cult' magazine and give one to Ron too. I've got two business ideas that could earn a million.

See you soon
God bless
Love
Reg

1981 April Montreal

Dear Kate could to tell
me so right
afternoon

But I will here to
tell it the
solicitor is

going to come
next day
Or he will
have to make it

Monday Morning

old beth
it will been ?

20 more tear,
oh more
since I met
my dear old
Peter.

HAHA
I will fet
your arse
missed it

Are not
Michael
Love Ron xx

19th April – Ron Kray

Dear Kate

Come and see me on Thursday afternoon but check here to
see if the solicitor is going to come that day or we will have
to make it Wednesday morning.

My old Dutch. It has been 20 more years or more since I met
my Old Dutch. Ha Ha you will get your arse smacked if you
are not careful.

Love
Ron

Monday 14th APRIL. 1989. Ron. Kray

① MY DEAR KATE. Y HOPE — ARE OK. AS TODAY. — LOOKED A BIT UPSET AS IF — WANTED to tell me Something BUT HELD IT BACK. Y WANT — to know WHAT Y THINK ter WORLD OF —. — ONLY WANT to tell — BE HAPPY.

Y DONT HAVE ALL WANT — DO FOR ME — REJ — TAKE IT ALL FOR GRANTED

Y AM VERY GREAT FULL — to — Ron

KATE CAN — GET MY GLASSES MADE WITH ter SAME TORTASHELL FRAMES AS YOUR PHILLIP DARK GLASSES HAVE GOT THANK —

KATE Y AM HAVING A LATE NIGHT TO NIGHT, Y AM LISTENING TO ROY ORTISON — ELVIS. PRESSLEY —

Y AM LOOKING FOR WARD to SEEING — ON FRIDAY, Y ALWAYS DO. PLEASE GIVE HARY OUR BEST WHEN YOU SEE HIM TAKE CARE PA

KATE Y KNOW WHAT Y CAN TRUST — WITH MY LIFE. — Y CANT SAY WHAT ABOUT A LOT OF PEOPLE ONLY —

WOT YOU — IN ALL — A FEW MORE PEOPLE

Y LOVE LIFE KATE — ENJOY EVERY SECOND OF IT

WELL KATE GOD BLESS — LOVE Ron Ron X X X X PQ

Y HOPE — HAVE A GOOD DAY WITH PAMELA

X X
X X
X X
X X
X X
X X
X X
X X

Monday 17th April 1989 – Ron Kray

My dear Kate

I hope you are OK as today as you looked a bit upset. As if
you wanted to tell me something. But held it back. I want
you to know that I think the world of you. And only want to
see you happy.
I don't take all what you do for me and Reg and young
Charlie for granted.
I am very grateful to you – PTO

Kate, can you get my glasses made with the same tortoise shell
frames as your thick dark glasses you have got. Thank you!

Kate I am having a late night tonight I am listening to Roy
Orbison and Elvis Presley. I am looking forward to seeing
you on Friday. I always do. Please give Harry my best
wishes.

Kate I know I can trust you with my life and I can't say that
about a lot of people.
I love life Kate and enjoy every second of it.

Well Kate – God bless
Love from Ron

I hope you have a good day with Pamela.

Reg Kray – Gartree Prison near Leicester

27th March, Monday night

Kate, thanks for phoning in tonight, glad you had a good visit with Ron and that he's seeing Steve.
I've had a good day in the sunshine and trained in my cell.
I honestly believe you are good for Ron. Also that you can help him to gain eventual release. All the more reason that you should instil it into Ron it is so important that he save his money.

28th March, Tuesday 6am

Just having a cup of tea, I'll do exercise soon and again when I go to the gym.
Poor old Percy never got much of a birthday today. It's Steve's on 1st April Saturday.

29th March, Wednesday 9.30am

Steve phoned to say he had a good visit with Ron. I received your letter. It was not exactly a mine of information about Steve was it?
Glad you spoke to Brad and Kim.
He is a lovable kid, and I know he has a crush on you.
You never do tell me much about your visits with Ron other than the fact you see him which I find a little annoying.

30th March, Thursday 6.30am

Percy was right pleased with gold glove. It was nice of you.
Pete is sending you a cheque for £400, so give Steve the balance.

Thanks God Bless
Love Reg

I loaned Brad
the photo of you in the water! Ha! Ha!

Reg Kray. Gartree Prison near Leicester

7th August 6am Sunday

Kate,

There was an old desolate castle, amongst the ruins. And a pond nearby. And a passing stranger stopped beside the pond and looked. Looked into the stillness of the pond and asked a question –

The pond replied "A thousand years have passed by since yesterday!"
That was an old chinese proverb, where one has to use one's imagination!

Imagine a grand castle that has seen better days. The ballroom dancing – the loving couples by the mill pond – gaiety – laughter. The pond has seen all these better days, and now all that remained was the great stillness!!

Somehow that little proverb sums up time as no other can. Kate you will find in time, I am a lover of beautiful words and Kahlil Gilbran stimulates my thoughts, hence my request would you order his book for me 'A Tear and a Smile'.

I've been awake since 4am and I just wrote to Nel Charles.

Reg Kray. Lewes

26th July Wednesday night

Kate. No I do not know what you mean by "Get the Drift"
Can you talk English and be more specific. I do not like
American terminology. It's best you be a quiet little lady if
you are to be Ron's ambassador.
You must not start trying to advise in politics with me, you
see I do not like anyone who tries to think for me. I value my
head too much.
Just thought I would let you know.
Keep smiling
Think of old Percy!
God Bless
Love Reg.

7th Nov '88

I just did my dynamic tension and other exercises step ups on chair etc.
I feel really bouncing with ideas today.
I create my own world in here with my thoughts early each day and so far today has been good to me.
It's right foggy outside my window. So I doubt if we will work. They do not take us out in the fog in case we get lost! Ha! Ha!

One time I had a good idea, I should have followed up. A pie and mash shop in the heart of Soho, cheap meals for all the tourists.

My pie and mash eaten from bowls with people sitting in cubicles with Dickens paintings round the wall. And I would have called the place "Sweenie Todds" after the barber who ate the dead bodies he murdered.
I would have had the story of "Sweenie Todd" on the menus and around the walls.
Let me know your thought. Soho is teaming with tourists.

God Bless
Love Reg.

Monday 21st Nov. Romsey

(1) DEAR KATE THANK —
for ALL — ARE
DOING for Reg —.
We don't take
it for
GRANTED

I am very GREAT full
to — KATE

(or BILL)

your friend
Romsey

Monday 21st Nov – Ron Kray.

Dear Kate, thank you for all you are doing for Reg and me.
I don't take it for granted.

I am very grateful to you Kate.
God Bless
From Your Friend
Ron Kray

ALSO BY KATE KRAY

HARD BASTARDS

Portraits of the twenty-four hardest men in Britain.
Price £14.99

NATURAL BORN KILLERS

Britain's eight deadliest murderers tell their own true stories.
Price £4.99

PRETTY BOY
by Roy Shaw

The bestselling autobiography of one of the hardest bastards
there is! Co-written by Kate.
Price £14.99

For your own copies, send off this coupon with cheque or credit card details to:

Blake Publishing Ltd.,
3 Bramber Court,
2 Bramber Road,
London W14 9PB

I would like to order:

.... *Hard Bastards* at £14.99 each (incl. p and p)

..........*Natural Born Killers* at £4.99 each (incl. p and p)

.... *Pretty Boy* at £14.99 each (incl. p and p)

EITHER

a. Debit my Visa/Access/Mastercard (delete as appropriate)

Card number ....

Expiry Date ..../..........

b. I enclose a cheque for .... made payable to Blake Publishing Ltd.

Name ....

Address ....

....

....

Daytime telephone ....

(Please allow 28 days for delivery)